FORGOTTEN

Scott A. Caughel

Pursuit of Character

Pursuit of Character

In Truth - By Faith - Through Grace

Our Logo represents the Source of Truth, the One in whom our Faith is placed, and the Grace by which we are saved.

The burning bush in the background represents God the Father, who is behind all, as He presented Himself to Moses (Exodus 3). Next comes the empty cross, which represents the sacrifice and victory of Christ, the Risen Son (John 3). In front is the fish, which represents God the Holy Spirit who Christ promised to send to teach and protect us (John 14). All are combined as One image: The Triune One.

This imagery is repeated in the images heading each chapter. The Heart, representing the Father's Love, the Cross, the Son's Victory (our Hope) and the Dove, the Spirit's presence.

Pursuit of Character

TABLE OF CONTENTS

About the Cover

The book is finished right down to the table of contents. I have had in mind, almost since the beginning, what I wanted the cover to represent and have found nothing that made that representation better than this photo. That said, I had never intended to write a section like this until this morning. I have been working on the cover for weeks now trying to get it to say exactly what I wanted it to say. This morning over coffee and our daily family reading time (currently, A.W. Tozer's book *A Divine Conquest*), it was suddenly made clear to me why this was the only image that would work.

You see, the person on the cover is my editor, Bethany, a God chosen member of our family. Bethany had a childhood we should all be thankful we did not have. Under the veil of "Christianity," she has suffered at the hands of Hypocrites, Heretics and Hirelings. But, through it all, she had Hope. I am told that while raised under this veil her entire life, in the midst of this darkness, she reached out to God. Through the darkness, still in her youth, she heard the Shepherd's call… and answered, "I want no more than to know You fully." Contrary to what you may have been told, the age of accountability is not a number in the physical construct of time but a state of Spiritual maturity that can distinguish between true right and wrong. Because she had reached that state and because her plea was sincere, God honored it.

In *A Divine Conquest*, Tozer talked about what Jacob had to go through to have his "self-will" broken so that he would be truly open to God's. The events I just described did not mean Bethany had it easy from that point out. In fact, most of what she would have to suffer and live through had not yet begun. As one of the seeds of Adam, she too would "stumble" through the battles, but her Shepherd would not leave her lost. Her Hope was guaranteed. The world would see her a "Victim," but her God would see her a "Victor."

Today, the veil has been torn asunder and she stands strong as a true image of her Creator in a world still filled with Hypocrites, Heretics and Hirelings. She is far from reaching full restoration of this image, as we all are, but in her, He has built His Church. In His Providence, He has used what the Adversary has brought down on her as a fire to Temper the steel of her soul and has placed her as a light in the darkness, as a representation of what embracing Hope looks like.

It occurs to me that there were two reasons this photo was "the" photo. The first I just described and the second I had not remembered until I sat down to write this. This photo was taken in 2016 on a road trip across the U.S. When it was taken, we were in sheep country. While staying at this particular stop, the rancher, our host, told us of his and the other ranchers' frustration. He said those with the authority up in the capital, people who had no idea of the subject, were continuing to write laws that increased the protection of the wolves. He told of countless sheep in countless pastures being lost (killed) because the wolves were being protected from the "shepherds." His representation of the decimation of the flock was jaw-dropping. The wolves had been let in the gate and the sheep were in constant danger in the very pastures where they once were safe. If you don't see the relevance of this now, you will before you finish this book.

To conclude, let me fill in the piece of the photo that was necessarily cropped out in the making of this cover. I took this photo as Bethany sat upon this rock watching the sunrise. Unbeknownst to Bethany, the sun was rising over seemingly endless pastures where the shepherd's sheep roamed. Also unbeknownst to her, the fact that these were the very same pastures where wolves lay in wait.

Preface

In education, there is a process used to decide the most effective course to facilitate student learning. Basically, you start with the result you want and work backward to discover the best place to start and the best path forward to reach that goal. This is the process I believe I have been under for a few years now. This process has produced more than 50 posts on the Pursuit of Character (P.O.C.) website and brought me to four posts that I did not publish. These posts seemed to be the culmination of all the posts. From their vantage point, I could turn around and look forward, back through all I had written before. This also caused another result I did not plan for or quite honestly want – "It's time to write a book… or books." So, here we are, and this is why you will see continuous excerpts from those posts tied into our discussion.

Also, let me note that I understand the world in its acceptance of Secular Morality has decided you can plagiarize yourself. Yes, I am told you can steal your own words. To the extent that this is true, be forewarned: I will use my own words. I will, without question, repeat myself. After all, if what we say isn't worth repeating, was it really worth saying in the first place? Let me state for the record: I give myself permission to use my words, current or past, as I see fit. Should I ever sue myself for using words, phrases or even paragraphs I have already published, I plead guilty and offer myself all I have as compensation. If you would like to see where I have used my words before I encourage you to read my entire website: www.PursuitOfCharacter.org

After the biographies provided at the end of the book, you will find an "About the Author" narrative. As with the biographies, reading it might help you understand what has brought me to bring these thoughts together and offer them to you.

Introduction

To those who find life desperate or just routine. To those who struggle to get out of bed or just can't seem to get to sleep. To those who believe there is no more and to those who ask, "Is this it?" **I point you to Hope!**

In the modern age, hope has become this empty thing we use to label our unlikely or shallow wishes. We throw it around with the flippancy of "How ya doin," "Nice to see you," or "Get well soon." The result? Hope has lost its meaning. The Truth Is, Hope is not empty. In fact, it would hold its own in a competition for the word with the most meaning. The problem is twofold: the world around us has done its best to hide or remove this Hope altogether and those who are supposed to trumpet it to the world have forgotten its true meaning.

In the chapters to come, we will re-introduce you to this Great Hope. We will discuss all the forces at work to keep it from us. We will shine our little light into the ever-present gray so you might see that, by comparison, this Hope is like stadium lights shining out in the darkest night. We will expose the lies that have sought to hide this Hope from us, and we will re-set the vocabulary the world has so gradually and cleverly re-defined.

Update:

Before the book is even published, I am including an update. In reality, Forgotten Hope should be in marketing and publication right now and, therefore, not open to this addition. However, the latest version of coronavirus, COVID-19, which has caused a global retreat, has delayed the final editing process. While this process has been negatively impacted, our family's daily reading, study, and devotion have not. As a result of these two realities, I have this one-hundred-year-old update to offer.

You may wonder why I use the Webster's 1828 dictionary as my reference source rather than something newer. You may also wonder why I look up and Re-Set seemingly obvious words. "For two full generations (the average time from birth to child-birth, considered approximately 20 years) the habit of emptying words of one meaning and refilling them with another has been taking place among the churches…" This was the subject of an article written 60+ years ago, "The Honest Use of Religious Words", by A.W. Tozer, and currently available in the book, *The Set of The Sail*.

While the content and approach of the P.O.C. website and Forgotten Hope shows that I have been aware of this problem and that the world had been implementing this strategy for a long time, we were surprised to see that it had already been this prevalent in Tozer's day. So prevalent in his lifetime that he identified the time when it was born: 100 years ago, the Adversary began the whisper, "re-defining the words we use was necessary, even thoughtful and loving." "The modern effort to popularize the Christian faith has been extremely damaging to that faith.…to simplify truth for the masses by using the language of the masses rather than the language of the church." Tozer goes on: "Positive beliefs are not popular these days. A mistaken desire to maintain a spirit of tolerance among all races (meaning cultures) and religions has produced a breed of Januslike Christians (Januslike meaning, acting in contrasting ways, duplicitous or two-faced)…The philosophy behind the whole thing is that religious beliefs are a matter of personal choice, and that the Lord adapts His saving truth to the individual, varying it to the cultural background, educational level and social situation of each one. What ever this is, it is not Christianity."

Tozer also provides a partial list of these re-defined words already identified in his time; "Inspiration', 'Revelation', 'Spiritual', 'Fellowship', 'Brotherhood', 'Unity', 'Worship', 'Prayer', 'Heaven', 'Immortality', 'Hell', 'Lord', 'New Birth', 'Converted'- but the list is long and includes almost every major word of the Christian faith." In his article, Tozer points out that the words written down by Moses, the Prophets and the Apostles mean what they meant when they wrote them and that when they wrote them, they were directed by God. Therefore, "We dare not be less than accurate in our treatment of anything so precious." As "The hope of the church yet lies in the purity of her theology, that is, her beliefs about God and man and their relation to each other."

So, there you have it: "All Scripture is God-breathed and is useful for instruction, for conviction, for correction, and for training..." But, as the Adversary could not attack this Truth directly, he has undermined it by "emptying" the meanings of the words contained. And, as Tozer made clear 60+ years ago, too many of today's churches and their members have adopted the Adversary's "refilling" of the words. Therefore, I look them up in the Greek and Hebrew dictionary. Then, I take what I find there, and I look that up in Webster's 1828. From there, I re-read the Instruction the Manual gives, listening for the Holy Spirit's Teaching. That, I pass along to you. – **end Update**

A great man dedicated his life to roving the country determined to "Revive" this Hope. This man, Vance Havner, said, "It's hard to be optimistic, with misty optics." We aim to clean those optics to give a clear look at "The Offer" of Hope. In so doing, we will present the warnings given against the things, the circumstances, and the people that would steal this Hope from us.

Please walk with me as I search through time for those who sought and fought to retain and revive this Hope. As we walk, you'll find that often these people will make their way between the quote marks on our journey and will be given proper credit for their inspiration. In fact, I again break the rules and do not dissuade you from jumping to the end of the book. I not only recommend but advise that you do just that. There, you will find brief biographies of these great people of God that may bring you a better understanding when they are referenced.

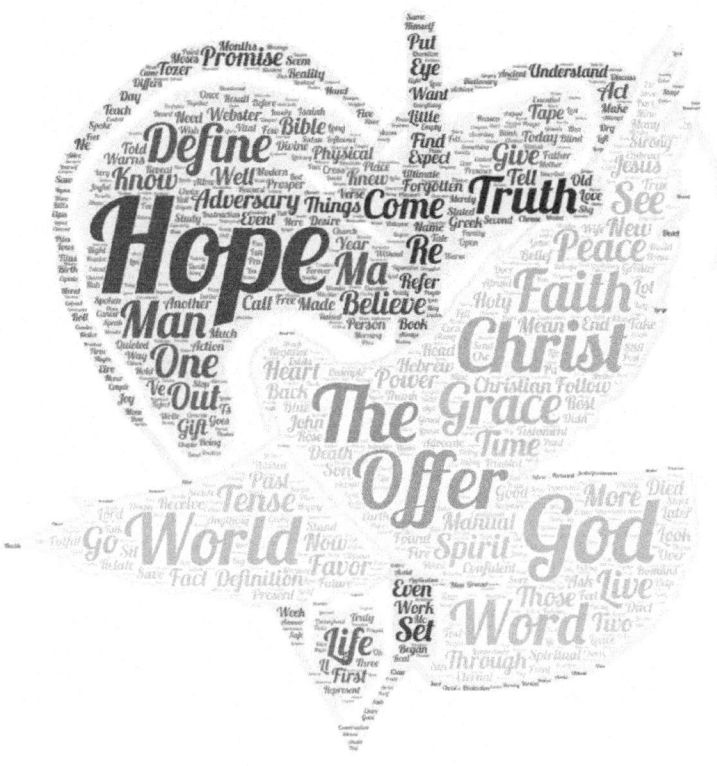

CHAPTER 1

Defining Hope & The Offer

I have been thinking a lot about **Hope** recently, and it weighed heavily on my heart that True Hope seems to have been forgotten. It also occurred to me that it is vitally important that I Trumpet the Truth about how Great this offer of True Hope is. How "to secure a good

Hope" was the message David M'Clure gave on New Year's 1799, and this is our goal as well. First, as promised, we should Re-Set the vocabulary. Hope is "to anticipate, usually with pleasure; expectation (abstract or concrete) or confidence: – faith, hope" at least in relation to the ancient Greek word "Elpis" as defined in Strong's Hebrew and Greek Dictionary. Webster's 1828 Dictionary defines hope as "Confidence in a future event; the highest degree of well-founded expectation of good." Webster's 1828 also says, "hope differs from wish and desire in this, that it implies some expectation of obtaining the good desired." So, there is the literary definition of hope, but the Hope we are talking about takes this definition and applies it to a much deeper meaning. Without this Hope, no real hope exists.

Hope is not empty or frivolous. As Webster says, it is not merely a wish or desire. This is what the world has reduced it to, but it is much more.

What is this Hope?

> "…as we await the blessed Hope…Jesus Christ." (Titus 2:13) "Christ Jesus our Hope." (1 Timothy 1:1) "Jesus will appear…in Him put (your) Hope." (Romans 15:12) Jesus Christ Himself said, "…I go and prepare a place for you, I will come back and welcome you into My presence…" (John 14:3)

This Hope is the fulfillment of a promise made by God 700 years earlier. Matthew stated so bluntly, "This was to fulfill what was spoken through the prophet Isaiah: In His name the nations will put their Hope." (Matthew 12:17, 21) Also, from Isaiah, "Behold, the virgin will be with child and will give birth to a son, and she will call Him Immanuel." (Isaiah 7:14) "He will stand and shepherd His flock in the strength of the LORD, in the majestic name of the LORD His God. And they will dwell securely, for then His greatness will extend to the ends of the earth. <u>And He will be their peace.</u>" (Micah 5:4,5) This **Hope** was planned on before creation, "…the Hope of eternal life, which God, who cannot lie, promised before time began." (Titus 1:2). "He has saved us and called us with a holy calling, not according to our works, but according to His own purpose and grace, which was given to us in Christ Jesus before time began." (2 Timothy 1:9) Let's tie this together with our literary definitions to reveal the forgotten definition of **Hope** Christ represents: **Hope Is** the joyful expectation of the fulfillment of what God promises. Or it might be said **Hope Is** the joyful expectancy of Faith. A world who would take away what God promises wants this **Hope** forgotten. This **Hope** threatens all that the Adversary's world works to achieve.

The Offer

It is really important to me that I represent this to you well. I am keenly aware that I or any other person am thoroughly inadequate to do The Offer of Hope and what Hope offers justice. **Christ is our Hope**… and what does Hope Offer? As always, I will refer you to the Manual and add a little personal experience with the belief that relating the application of Hope in my life will paint the clearest picture. In the words to follow, you will see me reference "the Physical" and "the Spiritual" worlds. Please pay particular attention to the distinctions made as they are vital to understanding The Offer and the ultimate reward of embracing The Offer.

My mother died unexpectedly on December 28, 2017. Ma had accepted The Offer of Hope a long time ago, and, on this day, she received the reward of that choice. Ma understood that The Offer was of a Truth greater than anything this Physical world could manifest. She knew God created her, Christ died for her, and Christ rose to open a door for her. This door was the only entrance to the Spiritual world, to the world of her Creator. Ma knew what we will discuss throughout this book; she knew Hope. Throughout her life, Ma flourished in fulfilling her responsibilities to The Offer in some parts and, like the rest of us, struggled in others. Through it all, she knew that Hope is an offer for Power in the world and not the power of the world. Ma knew that The Offer didn't promise this world would be better; it promised something much greater. Hope means "What Can Man Do To Me?"! Ma knew that peace may be offered by the Physical world but could never truly be delivered. Ma knew that True Peace comes from knowing that this world is only the blink of an eye and our existence is eternal. The Power of the Eternal Spiritual World has authority over this weak, temporary, Physical one. That is Hope, and from that Hope comes real peace.

So, I got the call that Ma had died. Later that night, when things calmed down and reality set in, the Adversary had his chance. As my mind quieted, sadness began to build. At that moment, I prayed that God would help me defeat my personal, physical sadness because I was so spiritually happy for Ma. When Pa had called me that morning, I immediately felt two things: my heart broke for Pa, but my spirit cheered for Ma. Quickly after finishing my prayer, I fell asleep and my dreams were filled with empty crosses and a line from a hymn. The next morning I awoke with the Peace and Joy I had requested. You see, while I would and still do miss the presence of Ma in my life, in those dawning hours, I knew God had fulfilled His Promise of Hope! Ma had received her reward! Ma had cashed in the reservation she had made the blink of an eye and a lifetime ago. Ma had received her salvation.

To give you complete context for what follows, I will inform you of another ongoing event in my life that started almost three years before Ma's death. I received some questionable test results. The question these results raised was, "Cancer?" For over five years now, this one test result has continued to get worse, exponentially raising my doctors' concerns. Many, many tests later they have not been able to find the C-Monster. I'm sure you can imagine the Physical world response these events invoke… or could invoke. Well, that's enough to set the stage. Now let me try to relate the Power of the Spiritual World.

In His Offer of Hope, Christ says, "Peace I leave with you; My peace I give to you. I do not give to you as the world gives. Let not your heart be troubled; neither let it be afraid." (John 14:27) The Power of the Spiritual World, God's World, over the Physical world is clearly represented in these few words.

Vocab-Re-Set:

In the Old Testament, the word used for this "Peace" was "shalom;" in the New Testament, it is "eirēnē." Strong's defines these words as follows:

shalom (shaw-lome) "safe, that is, (figuratively) well, happy, friendly; also (abstractly) welfare, that is, health, prosperity, Peace"

eirēnē (i-rah'-nay) "Peace (literally or figuratively); by implication prosperity: – one, peace, quietness, rest."

Christ verifies what I have said. His offer of Hope brings with it Peace. Not the false peace that the world offers, but True Peace. If you accept and embrace The Offer and the rules (we'll get to that), you will be **safe**, you will be **happy**, you will **prosper**. Follow Him and you will find **quietness** and **rest**. Christ's words end with, "Let not your heart be troubled; neither let it be afraid." But the original Greek word used was "may," defined as "that not" or "lest." In other words, **"I offer you Peace that your heart will not be troubled and that you will not be afraid."**

As I have grown in my understanding of The Offer and the promise that goes with it, I have received Peace. **This Peace has grown as I have learned to "Live In" or of the Spiritual world and in but "Not Of" the Physical.** With the death of my mother, I was at **Rest.** In the five years pursuing the potentially cancerous cause of continuing bad test results, I have been **Happy.** I found **Quietness** when my wife was told she needed immediate open-heart surgery. Three weeks later, when she was told, "Never mind, there is nothing wrong with your heart. You have your health." I had **Peace.** While the physical world piles on the medical bills from these events, I know **Prosperity.** With the death of another immediate family member (my wife's sister), **my heart is Not Troubled.** I look forward to an endless future Living In Christ's house and **I am Not Afraid.** With this understanding, you will find the Truth of which He spoke. You can find safety and prosperity that is of the Physical World, but that is nothing to the Safety and Prosperity that Christ offers. When you live with Hope, you will see that the wealthiest person of the world is a pauper compared to the Prosperity promised by Christ.

I mentioned my wife's life and death heart issue… that happened on August 19, 2018, at 2:30 AM. On August 17, 2018, at 7:00 PM we had just moved the last of our things to our new home. This home is the home we had been praying for our entire lives, but it was going to require a lot of upkeep, i.e. a lot of work. I also mentioned that my wife was cleared three weeks later (miracle anyone?). That was a Thursday.

On Sunday morning, as we began – and I mean just began – to prepare for the carpet installer to arrive, I put my back out. Not just a little out. I couldn't get out of bed for weeks. Nine months later, I almost recovered twice; meaning, my back went out two more times over those nine months, the first time while I slept. I'm guessing you've realized my contributions to this new, large commitment have been practically non-existent. As my family will attest, I am someone with a very low boredom threshold and an over-assertive need to do-for-myself. OK, you've got the picture.

I hope (little h) that my personal experience has helped you to understand and maybe even begin to relate to The Offer of Hope (Big H) you have been given. The World isn't getting any better… and that doesn't have to be your problem. The Adversary is out there… and you don't have to be afraid. If you ever have to face cancer, or even the possibility like me, wouldn't it be nice if you had the Peace to say, "Do what you will. If the eviction notice comes, I have a mansion waiting."?

I thank God every day that He answered my prayer on December 28, 2017. I thank God for **Peace** eight months later through a time that previously would have stressed me to no end. Nine months after that, I thank God for **Quietness** in a time of Physical world attacks where my **Heart was Not Troubled.** Today, I thank God for **Hope**, and I look forward to an endless future as part of the Spiritual Kingdom of God.

The Offer Stands

To those who found your way to the church looking for what I've described, that exciting skydive, but found the church was just as stuck on the ground as you, **I point you to Hope!** For those who thought God would feel more like a warm, submersing swim, but find yourself dry, **that experience is out there… Hope!** If you know or even feel like you might be standing in a burning building and can't see through the smoke, the Firefighter has come, **have Hope!**

Let's be clear. **This Hope Is Christ.** This Hope is not Past-Tense. This does explain, however, why the Modern Christian and the church they attend are dry and stuck on the ground. The very people who are supposed to know, live and represent Hope no longer offer it as intended. Sure, most Modern Christians believe in Christ, but the Christ they believe in is Past-Tense. Christ lived, died and rose to sit at the right hand of God. Because of this, the hope they offer is firmly anchored in Past-Tense. But that is not what The Offer says! This Offer of Hope uses words like "is" and "sits" and even future-tense like "ask" and "will." Here are a couple of examples from The Offer:

> "I will not leave you as orphans; I will come to you." John 14:18

> "…I will ask…and He will give you another Advocate to be with you forever…" John 14:16

A Modern Christian will likely say, "Sure, I believe in all that, but…"

I once heard a sermon from Tozer where he attempted this issue. While making the case, he laughed at himself a little because even his habit, like ours, was to speak in the Past-Tense. The point he wanted to make was that we should use "is" or "says" but we use "was" or "said" instead. The message of the sermon was that the Scriptures were written by The Holy Spirit through men of God. Being God, the Holy Spirit is eternal, "yesterday, today, and forever;" therefore, we should say Paul says, not Paul said, because it is the Spirit speaking, not Paul, and His Words, His Instruction, His Offer is Present-Tense.

Jump ahead from Tozer sixty years and we're back at "a Past-Tense Christ." Christ is God. Christ is Eternal. But it is essential to The Offer, to Hope, that we understand more about Christ. Christ is the Son of Man. This means God as Christ broke down the walls between the Spiritual and Physical worlds and was born as a man, the second Adam. Then, the man Christ died on the cross, and the man Christ returned from the dead. In between, having put in place the new opportunity for individual men to choose, Christ the Son of God and Man went and took the keys of the power of death and Hell from the Adversary. God in the form of man tore down the walls on the opposite side, moving from the Physical world back to the Spiritual world to the "outer darkness" where Lucifer had been cast. This act put in place the coinciding outcomes of that individual choice… God or the Adversary, Heaven or Hell. Then, the Son Christ with His "Entire Being," (Physical and Spiritual as one) walked out of the tomb. The man did not evaporate and the Spirit float out. Scripture says the cover stone rolled away and broke and the Son of God, that is Christ, rose off of the stone slab and walked out. It also says that Christ walked with a chosen few for another forty days. Then, Christ as the Risen Man ascended into Heaven and "sits," present-tense, at the right hand of God.

Many, maybe even most, will defend and say, "That's exactly what I believe." But is it? Why are your feet stuck on the ground? Today, the average "Christian" sees the Bible as more of a historical document… you know, Past-Tense. Even worse than being referred to in Past-Tense, the Bible has been diminished to merely stories for another time and place. Have you ever heard anything like, "Abraham, Moses, Elijah, etc. lived in a different time when God's power was more prominent." Or "Angels spoke directly to men. God Himself not only spoke to Moses, He spent forty days hanging out with him on a mountain… that just doesn't happen today." And "Yes, there was a time when God was a man, and that man not only healed the sick, he raised the dead… but that was Christ. That power went with Him when He left." These examples may seem extreme, but some version of them is being spoken every moment by some "Christian" somewhere. Well, there's the undeniable belief the Modern Christian will deny they have. Christ offered Hope. Christ offered something more powerful than anything the world could offer. But that was then. Today, Christ is that warm fuzzy feeling in a world where no one is judged and all are welcome.

So, that's the problem; back to the solution… back to Hope! Christ Is! "Truly, truly, I tell you, whoever believes in Me <u>will</u> also do the works that I am doing. He <u>will</u> do even greater things than these, because I am going to the Father. And I <u>will</u> do whatever you <u>ask</u> in My name, so that the Father may be glorified in the Son. If you ask Me anything in My name, I <u>will</u> do it." (John 14:12 – 14) "Will" is Future-Tense. Christ said that after He ascended to the right hand of God, you will do greater things than He did. Christ says if you believe in Him, He will do anything you "ask," Present-Tense.

Christ Is, the power of God Is – **There's your Hope!** Christ didn't just live, Christ Lives – **There's your Hope!** "I will not leave you as orphans; I will come to you." (John 14:18) **There's your Hope!** "If you love Me, you will keep My commandments. And I will ask the Father, and He will give you another Advocate to be with you forever…" (John 14:15,16) **There's your Hope!** (Quick note about "anything" for the "Materialist." It says, "the works that (He) is doing" and "that the Father may be Glorified.")

God's power did not belong to or come from Moses. Christ is not Past-Tense. When on Earth, Christ did greater things than Moses, and He promises that we can do greater things than He did while on Earth. Christ says that for those who "follow His commandments," God will send an "Advocate." Christ goes on to say that this Advocate "…is the Spirit of Truth." Christ also warns that "The world cannot receive Him, because it neither sees Him nor knows Him." This is not a negative statement… it is a positive warning that to live as the Physical world is to reject Christ, not to "Love" Him. Let's take a look at that for a second. I understand that looking at the faults in today's Christianity can feed the incorrect narrative that God is a God of negatives and the Bible a book of don'ts. Allow me to illustrate: "swimming is wonderful and fun, but don't jump into the lake wearing snow boots and a winter coat." Or "Skydiving is an exhilarating, exciting, once in a lifetime experience, but don't jump out of the plane without a parachute!" One more… "If you find yourself caught in a burning building, run to the firefighter if you want to live. Don't run further into the flames." It seems obvious that in the first two examples great opportunities are presented. It is also obvious that, along with those opportunities, warnings are offered of things you could do that would cost you the joy of those opportunities. Would anyone say those "don'ts" were negatives? The last example presents you with the choice of life or death. The warning tells you what action leads to death and not to do it if you want to live. Is there any way to see that as a negative? So, along with The Offer of Hope comes warnings, but those who see these as negatives are "blind to the Truth." We'll elaborate on that later. For now, I want to focus the reader on the amazing opportunity, the exciting experience, the lifesaving offer God presents.

While a worldly life blinds you to the Truth, to God, to Christ and the Holy Spirit, Christ says that the Spirit "…will teach us All things…" (John 14:26). Romans 8:26 tells us that "…the Spirit helps us in our weakness," and that "…the Spirit Himself intercedes for us…" Christ says that He died for our "benefit" and that if He didn't, the "Advocate," the Holy Spirit, would not have been sent. "I tell you the truth, it is for your benefit that I am going away. Unless I go away, the Advocate will not come to you; but if I go, I will send Him to you." (John 16:7) The Manual points to the Fire and says, "Don't run into the flames! Come to the Firefighter, Christ, and He will save you!" Then, after He saves you, He will send a Protector for you. This Protector will teach you to avoid the fire and He will "…make intercession (with God for us) with inexpressible groanings."

Not only is Christ Not "Past-Tense," the greatest gifts God has for man came since Christ's death: Salvation, Rebirth with Christ, and the "indwelling" of the Holy Spirit. Because Christ "Is," Salvation "Is." Because Christ "Is," the Holy Spirit "Is" offered to those who "Love Christ." It's time Christians stop teaching History Lessons and start living a Present Christ Life. Havner said, "Give me a band of people who live as if Jesus died yesterday, Rose this morning and is coming back tonight." If **Hope!** is **Forgotten**, it's because we stopped demanding it from ourselves and stopped offering its True meaning to the world.

Allow me to relay this offer to you… Christ Is alive today and offers us more than when He walked this earth. Christ has a plan, not only to save you from the fire but to provide you a Teacher and Protector who can defeat whatever the Adversary throws at you. We may have "Forgotten Hope!" but thank God He hasn't. **Christ Is our Hope! He Is alive today and His Offer Stands!**

The Adversary

As you read, you see me continuously reference the Bible as the Manual, but the world spins it to say it is a book of negatives. This is an obvious tale from the Adversary. Why does he tell this tale? Because the Bible is also a Fire Safety Manual. These so-called "negatives" are warnings on how to avoid the Fire and how to get out if you are caught in it. Let us not forget, the Adversary is the chief Arsonist.

The Adversary, in his cleverness, has used the world to re-define our vocabulary, re-write Scripture and re-characterize the Bible. In our weakness, Christians have embraced the Adversary's work and teach something less than what God prescribes. So, I follow Christ's example and attempt to use mental imagery to combat this damage and Re-Set our perspective. Every time you read the word "Manual," I am attempting to get you to reject the Adversary's heresy and read the Bible for what it is… an "Instruction Manual." I use Adversary for the same reason I described using Manual. Every time you read it, I want you to have the mental image of your enemy, of the one who would steal your **Hope**, of your Adversary… Satan.

I am not going to devote a lot of "ink," as they say, to the Adversary. Although it is critical to understand him, he is represented all through our discussion and I am not going to add distinction above that. "Adversary" is the definition of the Hebrew word "saw-tawn." (Strong's, "saw-tawn': an opponent; especially Satan, the arch-enemy of good: - adversary.") You can see where "Satan" comes from. Webster's 1828 defines Adversary as, "An enemy or foe; one who has enmity at heart… An opponent or antagonist…Opposed; opposite to; adverse." So, there you have it. The Adversary is everything contrary; just as sin is anything not good, the Adversary is everything contrary to that same good. He is darkness, lies, and immorality. He is a thief, a wolf, and a trickster. He is everything God is not and everything that should be avoided.

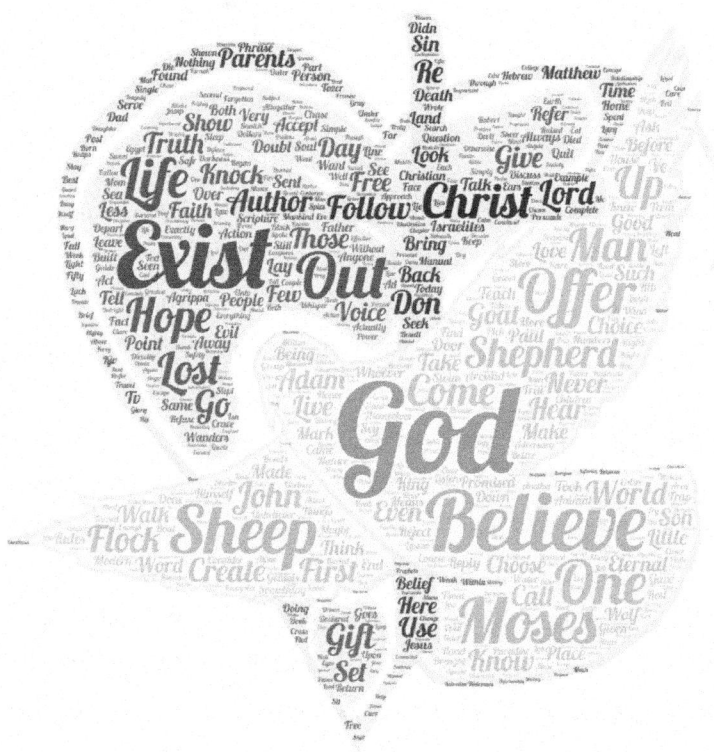

CHAPTER 2

He Is & He Calls

So, there's The Offer. There's the Forgotten Hope. But, as you will see, I am a big believer in "application." If Hope Is "the joyful expectancy of Faith," what are we to expect? In what or Who is our Faith? To answer this requires a little more Vocab Re-Set. I literally spent months researching the "old" meaning of three words. When I was done, I wanted to communicate them in a new way, or at least in a way that, along with Hope, may have been forgotten. It is essential that you know what I found because the foundation of all I write is **"In Truth, By Faith, and Through Grace."**

It wasn't long after I started writing posts for my website that the need to study and define key language became obvious. From this need developed what would become the "Is Series." As I explain in the first of the series, "Truth Is," this need threw itself at me in a couple of events. The first was during a political season where the media offered a set of facts and then a Presidential staffer offered "alternative facts." The second was from a conversation that was related to me where the person on the other end said they "stand with the truth." They followed this statement with "the truth they believe." These events made me wonder, "What is truth? Can there be "alternate" versions? Does what I "believe" matter? More importantly, how does God define Truth?" To answer these questions, I dove into a two-week plus study of "the Manual." I cross-referenced the Greek and Hebrew dictionary, Webster's 1828 dictionary and several more translations of the Manual. In brief, this is what I found.

Truth Is

The Greek word for Truth is alétheia. It is defined as follows: "truth, but not merely truth as spoken; truth of idea, reality, sincerity, truth in the moral sphere, divine truth revealed to man, straightforwardness" (Strong's). Ancient Greek culture used alétheia to mean "reality." To them, Truth was not a belief or an opinion but a fact. This is a good start. Truth, as used in the Manual, is "Divine Truth," <u>facts</u> revealed to man by God. This is Truth not merely spoken but undeniable Reality.

I went on in the post to quote various Scriptures that demonstrate all Truth has an ultimate Truth and that ultimate Truth is defined by God's moral Authority. For Christians, for those wanting to take God up on His Offer of Hope, this Truth is strewn throughout the Scriptures. And, as we have already stated, the Bible is the Word written by The Holy Spirit, the Bible is Truth, the Truth is present-tense, and the Truth is unquestionable. Let me give you a quick example. Look up; the sky is blue. Now, a person who has been blind since birth has no concept of color, so they don't know what blue is. The fact that they cannot see it does not change the Truth that it is blue. Now, a free spirit comes along and decides, I don't believe in blue, so I'm going to believe the sky is orange. What they choose to believe doesn't matter, ultimately there is one Truth, the sky is blue. So, in the events that inspired this Truth quest, I don't know whether the politician or the media told the truth or if it fell somewhere in between. What I do know is that, in the end, there was only one Truth, and whether either one of them was telling it or believing it or not didn't matter. In Reality, the Truth is… "Truth Is."

Faith Is

Why did I go into that whole spiel on Truth? Two reasons. First, if we don't accept the fact that Truth Is, then we've taken God out of The Offer, and, the Truth Is, without God there is no offer. The second reason is the second post in the Is Series, "Faith Is." I put the same kind of study into Re-Setting the definition of this word, and, after all that work, a family member read to me from Tozer's book *The Pursuit of God*. Here's what she read: "Outside of a brief fourteen-word (KJV) definition in Hebrews 11:1, I know of no biblical definition." He goes on in the rest of the chapter to discuss "Faith Is" under the following understanding: "…we drop the notion of definition and think about faith as it may be experienced in action." Leave it to Tozer to offer in a couple of sentences what I took two weeks to discover. I want to show you what Hebrews 11:1 says, "Now faith is confidence in what we hope for and assurance about what we do not see."

Two words in Hebrews 11:1 struck me: Confidence and Assurance. What do these words mean? Webster's 1828 defines confidence as: "firm belief in the integrity, stability or veracity of another, or in the truth and reality of a fact." And assurance as: "full confidence or trust; freedom from doubt; certain expectation; the utmost certainty." The following two verses make the connection to Truth Is: "This is why the ancients (elders) were commended. By faith we understand that the universe was formed by God's command, so that what is seen was not made out of what was visible." (Hebrews 11:2&3) How do we know this Truth? As Robert Boyle said, "…only because God told us." "In the beginning God created the heavens and the earth." (Genesis 1:1) If He made it all, He is the ultimate Authority on what Truth Is.

Tozer and I agree that Hebrews 11:1 is the only place the Manual defines Faith. Unlike Tozer, in my efforts to understand Faith I do not "drop the notion of definition" but embrace it as essential for "action." So, what did I find the definition of Faith to be? "The firm belief in God's Truth or Reality of fact, free from doubt with utmost certainty about what we do not see. In other words, not just belief in God and the Hope that Christ brings, but absolute confidence in both." I believe this is why Faith is only defined once. The definition is passive, but, in Biblical terms, Faith Is a verb, or, as Tozer states, an action.

Allow me this illustration. Faith is Duct Tape, or as you may know it "Duck Tape." What is Duct Tape? Duct tape is a strong cloth fiber with strong waterproof adhesive backing, heat resistant, can hold where other tapes don't. This is what Duct Tape is while still wrapped in cellophane sitting on the store shelf. Left on the roll, Duct Tape is still all those things but what use are they? What will it hold together? What will it waterproof against? How strong does it have to be? The virtues and value of Duct Tape are only realized when action is taken to apply it. It is the action or application that truly defines Faith as well.

To sum-up, what I learned about Faith is this, **Faith Is** a verb! **Faith Is** action! **Faith Is** unyielding confidence! **Faith Is** walking in Truth! **Faith Is** to patiently endure, living life in God's Truth, confident that we "will receive what He has promised." What I discovered in my studies was Faith and Truth have an interesting bond. Truth is the divine word of God in us through Christ, and Faith is a proven devotion or obedience to that Truth that can only be achieved through Christ, our Hope.

This brings us to the How. If Truth and Faith are the what, then the How is Grace.

Grace Is

"You are all children of God through faith in Christ Jesus." (Galatians 3:26) "Therefore, the promise comes by faith, so that it may rest on grace and may be guaranteed…" (Romans 4:16)

I will begin where my study finished. Defined by Webster's 1828, Grace: "the free unmerited love and favor of God…" The Old Testament refers to this Grace as "God's Favor." In fact, most translations other than KJV have replaced the word Grace with Favor. In the Old Testament, however, there are two Hebrew words used for Grace. From Strong's, "Chên: graciousness, that is, subjectively (kindness, favor) or objectively (beauty): – favor, grace (-ious), pleasant, precious, [well-] favored." And "Techinnâh: graciousness; causatively entreaty: – favor, grace, supplication." Except for in the book of Ezra, the first word is always used. Chên refers to being seen with Favor in God's eyes. For example, Genesis 6:8: "But Noah found grace (chên) in the eyes of the LORD." The only other use of the word "Grace" in the Old Testament is in Ezra 9:8 and is translated from the word, techinnâh: "But now for a brief moment grace (techinnâh) has been shown by the LORD our God, to leave us a remnant and to give us a secure hold within his holy place, that our God may brighten our eyes and grant us a little reviving in our slavery." So, why the difference this one time? This verse refers to an act of Favor by God. Verse 9 then says, "…He has granted us new life." God's gift, the act of Grace, was empowerment, or, as the NASB puts it, a "reviving." This slight but important difference sets the stage for the New Testament use of Grace and how an <u>act</u> of God's Grace gave man access to the power of God… access to Hope.

The New Testament uses the word "charis" when referring to Grace. Here is the Strong's definition of this Greek word for Grace, "charis: graciousness (as gratifying), of manner or <u>act</u> (abstract or concrete; literal, figurative or spiritual; especially the <u>divine influence</u> upon the heart, and its reflection in the life; including gratitude): – acceptable, benefit, favor, <u>gift</u>, grace (-ious), joy liberality, pleasure, thank (-s, -worthy)."

Notice, similar to the word for grace used in Ezra, this definition speaks to "acts," "gifts" and "influence." Webster goes on to define Grace as: "Favorable influence of God; divine influence or the influence of the spirit" and "The application of Christ's righteousness to the sinner." What does this New Testament Grace look like? "We believe it is through the Grace (charis) of our Lord Jesus that we are saved…"

(Acts 15:11) "Through Him and on behalf of His name, we received Grace..." (Romans 1:5) Also, "...for all have sinned and fall short of the glory of God and are justified (made righteous) freely by His Grace through the redemption that is in Christ Jesus." (Romans 3:23,24) Finally, because it points directly to the forgotten Hope, "...the gift is not like the trespass. For if the many died by the trespass of the one man (Adam), how much more did God's Grace and the Gift that came by the Grace of the one man, Jesus Christ (our Hope), abound to the many!" (Romans 5:15) The "one man" Adam chose to reject Truth and so ushered in sin; because of the Gift of Christ, we are not bound by that decision. Verse 17 says we can choose Truth for ourselves. We can choose Hope and, in so doing, "reign in life through the one man, Jesus Christ!" Well, that's it. **Grace Is** Favor in the eyes of God, and **Grace Is** Acts of God (Gifts) freely given from that Favor. From that Grace, we are offered Hope!

He Exists

Havner taught that "Faith is not to believe that God can, Faith is to believe that God Will." We just discussed how such a Faith is shown in Action. Here's the problem: You can't believe He will if you do not first believe He Is. Hebrews 11:6 lays a little groundwork for our Offer of Hope: "...anyone who approaches Him must believe that He exists." The obvious inference is that we must first believe that He exists. Unfortunately, in our day, Believe is another word for which the true meaning has been forgotten. To the Modern Christian, Believe has become quite the lazy term. To some, you don't actually have to "Believe" to be a Believer; belief in the concept of God is enough. But that is not what The Offer says.

While I was studying for the post "The Salvation Myth," our family read a sermon given by Tozer at Wheaton College in 1952. The sermon, "The Danger of being Almost Altogether," was built on Acts 26:28,29: "Then (King) Agrippa said unto Paul, 'Almost you persuade me to be a Christian.' And Paul said, 'I would to God, that not only you but also all that hear me this day, were both almost, and altogether such as I am, except these bonds.'" (KJV) Paul, in his chains (bonds) for proclaiming Christ as the Messiah, had just made his defense to the king, reminding him of the king's "Belief in the prophets." Paul pointed out to the king that everything he had said came directly from the prophets and Moses. He simply showed and declared how Christ is the fulfillment of those same prophecies. Agrippa replied, "You've Almost convinced me." Was it 95%? 98%? We don't know. We just know it was almost. In other words, he almost believed that Christ is who He said He is. Paul replies, "Don't almost believe. Believe completely (Altogether)." Sadly for Agrippa, he never got to the 100% point of believing **God Is Exactly Who He says He Is**, that **He Exists as He defines Himself**. As Tozer points out, "When Agrippa used the word "almost," he did not know it at the time, but he had committed the greatest moral blunder of his life. History shows that the man's blunder was fatal. Shipwrecks, earthquakes, tidal waves, epidemics and all the rest – nothing compares in sheer unrelieved tragedy with the soul that has seen the cross and turned away from it…" The soul that has been offered Hope and rejected it. The Israelites spent their entire lives bouncing around in that few percent of doubt. As a result, an entire generation could not enter the Promised Land. "These things took place as examples to keep us from craving evil things as they did." (1 Corinthians 10:6) They were a walking illustration of this kind of "infidelity," of how being Almost a Believer reaps the same rewards as an Unbeliever outright.

Let's try a few examples of what to believe something exists looks like in application. A person walks up to you and offers you a million dollars to quit your job and go work for them. If you believe the million dollars exists, you very likely do as they ask. If you don't, you might laugh in their face and walk away from the offer. Here's another, maybe a little closer to something you've experienced. A week before Black Friday you hear an ad offering the first fifty people in line at the local department store a free TV. If you believe that the store exists, that the offer is real and you want a free TV, you might be one of those people sleeping on the sidewalk the night before. Here's one we use around our house. Say you're out on a boat in the middle of a deep lake and far from land. If you believe you can swim, you happily jump in to escape the heat. If you believe you will drown, that you can't swim good enough to stay above water, you will sweat it out on the boat. You might go around telling people you can swim, but what you truly believe is shown in your action. There is no gray area; we act on and in what we believe.

As Agrippa showed, anything less than complete, confident belief is unbelief. Any doubt in what God says or The Offer of Hope He makes rejects The Offer. Both generations of Israelites demonstrated this. The first sent out spies to verify what God had promised. Upon hearing the reports, they doubted the God of Moses and rejected the offer of paradise. In so doing, they were sent "wandering" never to be allowed in. Upon their return to the paradise God had promised, the second generation doubted that what God had promised could be better than what they had and were chastised by Moses for their lack of Faith (active belief in God's Truth). In reply, they bartered away paradise and would never receive what God had offered. Numbers says that "The Lord's anger burned..." because "...they did not follow Him completely." (Numbers 32:13, 12) The good news of these events? There were a few who believed God was who Moses said He was, who believed God was who He said He was and believed He spoke the Truth. These few whose actions showed they believed, who had Faith, were seen with favor in God's eyes and received the reward God had promised.

I think the world and the Modern Christian have fallen to a place that I need to take a minute and talk about Moses. The Truth we have set out to show is that to believe in The Offer you must believe in the Truth of the one who makes The Offer. To believe the Truth that He Exists, you must believe Moses. Christ said, "If you had believed Moses, you would believe Me, <u>because he wrote about Me</u>. But since you do not believe what he wrote, how will you believe what I say?" (John 5:46,47) So, here are the highlights. Moses was born a Hebrew at a time when to be so was a death sentence. He was hidden away as a baby and found by the Pharaoh's daughter. Moses was not a dumb man. Moses was raised with all the benefits and education such a station would offer. Jumping ahead, Moses was chosen by God to confront the powers of Egypt that had been his home and to free the enslaved Hebrews. Through this process and in the decades to follow, God talked directly to Moses. In fact, God spent forty days on Mount Sinai talking with and teaching Moses. God Himself buried Moses. "Moses the servant of the LORD died there in the land of Moab, as the LORD had said. And He buried him in a valley in the land of Moab facing Beth-peor..." (Deuteronomy 34:5,6)

Why the brief history lesson on Moses? We must "<u>First</u> Believe that He Exists" as He says He exists. Moses took dictation from God and immortalized His words in the first five books of the Bible. "In the beginning God created the heavens and the earth." (Genesis 1:1) "Then the LORD God formed man from the dust of the ground and breathed the breath of life into his nostrils, and the man became a living being." (Genesis 2:7) "...the LORD God took the man and placed him in the Garden of Eden." (Genesis 2:15) "...the LORD God caused the man to fall into a deep sleep, and while he slept, He took one of the man's ribs and closed up the area with flesh. And from the rib that the LORD God had taken from the man, He made a woman and brought her to him." (Genesis 2:21,22)

Do you believe Moses? Do you believe Moses got his information from the source of Truth? Do you believe God? Do you believe He Exists exactly as He says He Exists? Or do you believe less? Maybe only a little less? Maybe 2 or 3% less? Maybe you believe modern man can "theorize" better than Moses could hear? Christ Himself said in Mark 1:15 "believe in the gospel!" He didn't say to believe in parts of the Gospel. He simply said The Gospel. In fact, Christ constantly responded to questions or challenges with, "What did Moses command you?" (see Mark 10:3 for example). The Truth Is, if you throw away or tweak even a little of the Manual, the rest goes with it, including The Offer of Hope. "Whoever keeps the whole Law but stumbles at just one point is guilty of breaking all of it." (James 2:10)

A couple of quotes from the scientist, Robert Boyle: "...the World is the great Book, not so much of Nature, as of the God of Nature, which we should find crowded with instructive Lessons, if we had but the Skill, and would take the Pains, to extract and pick them out." And, "I am persuaded, that nature will be found very loyal to her Author, and instead of alienating his mind from making religious acknowledgments, will furnish him with weighty and uncommon motives, to conclude such sentiments to be highly rational and just." From the same Robert Boyle writing as a theologian: "We should obtain our opinions from Scripture rather than take them to Scripture since Scripture is the best expositor of itself." And "I am confirmed in the belief, that by transferring our impressions to the Sacred Text, we often impute to the Scriptures our own faults and deficiencies."

It's simple really. If you don't believe God can "create," then you can't believe He can "re-create." If God can't re-create, **there goes your Hope!** If you don't believe God has the power to speak the first Adam into existence, then you can't believe He could place the second Adam in Mary's womb. If you don't believe God brought Adam to life, then you can't believe He could bring Christ back to life. If you don't believe that… **there goes your Hope!**

One more lesson from the Israelites. Do you think atheist scientists were the first to do the bidding of the Adversary? To walk beside those who would follow God and whisper the Adversary's lies in their ears? "Then the foreign multitude who were traveling with the Israelites began to crave the good things of Egypt. And the people of Israel also began to complain." (Numbers 11:4) When God used Moses to free the Israelites, He also freed a lot of other slaves. These unbelievers "Grumbled" against Moses' God and the Israelites fell for the trap and adopted their doubt. As Boyle points out, "Sin came into the world by the weakness of one man, listening to the words of the devil…" Considering this approach has been so effective through the centuries, why would he ever give it up? And, considering this approach has been so effective through the centuries, why would we ever let our guard down against his whispers?

He Knocks

"…to secure a good Hope… of eternal life." This is how M'Clure's quote ends. This is what acceptance of The Offer brings. God says, "Behold, I stand at the door and knock. If anyone hears My voice and opens the door, I will come in…" (Revelation 3:20) Christ stands at the door to your heart; with Him, He brings The Offer of Hope. Hope of "eternal life." This Offer is the cure for our current course. A course set by Adam and followed by every person unless they accept The Offer. This course is one of eternal death. I think too many in this world believe the choice to be God or nothing, but this is not true. The choice is God or something, and that something is eternal death. Eternity without the presence of God. From the very beginning of this physical world, mankind was given this choice. God planted the tree of the knowledge of good and evil and He gave Adam a Gift. Adam was given the Gift of choice and the choice was simple: God or not God. Honor his Maker's instruction or defy Him and eat from the tree. I'm sure some would say God set a trap for Adam. But Free Will is not a trap, it is a Gift. If we have nothing to choose between then no choice can be made and Free Will does not exist. Even though He could have left Adam with no choice, God so loved Adam (and us) that He wanted Adam to choose to Love Him.

God knew before Adam was even created that he and we would make bad choices. He could have said, "I won't allow mankind not to choose Me. I will leave Free Will out of the design." But He didn't. His love went one step farther. He said, "I will create mankind with the ability to choose, and because I know they will choose not to listen, I will give them a chance to change their answer… I will give them Hope." "For God so loved the world that He gave His one and only Son…" (John

3:16) God planned on Christ to offer us Life Anew before a single choice, a single sin had occurred. Christ "…was known before the creation of the world." (1 Peter 1:20) "…the Son of Man did not come to be served, but to serve, and to give His life as a ransom for many." (Mark 10:45)

Christ says, "Come, follow Me." (Mark 1:17) Today, the Modern Christian seems to think Christ will chase after them or that He introduces Himself and then says, "I will see you at the finish line." They are wrong. When was the last time you chased someone down who had fled your presence just so you could give them a gift? What would you think if you gave someone who stopped by your house a gift and, after thanking you, they said, "I'm really busy going forward. Could you bring it by my place at the end of the month?" I'm pretty sure few would find either scenario acceptable. When a gift is offered, a person chooses to either accept it or refuse it. If the gift is refused, it is unreasonable to believe the giver will chase you down and force it on you. Also, to accept a gift, you must actually take possession of it. Otherwise, the gift is not yet yours. So, Christ Knocks on the door and says, "I have a Gift for you. I Offer you Hope. Hear My voice, open the door and come follow Me."

This is a plate my mother (Ma) had either hanging or sitting around the living room longer than I can remember. It was one of her most treasured objects for what it represented.

He knocks… and says, "…whoever welcomes Me welcomes not only Me, but the One who sent Me." Mark 9:37

He knocks… and says, "I am the bread of life. Whoever comes to Me will never hunger, and whoever believes in Me will never thirst." John 6:35

He Knocks… and says, "If anyone is thirsty, let them come to Me and drink. Whoever believes in Me, as the Scripture has said: 'Streams of living water will flow from within them.'" John 7:37, 38

He knocks… and says, "I am the light of the world. Whoever follows Me will never walk in the darkness, but will have the light of life." John 8:12

He knocks… and says, "It is My Father's will that everyone who looks to the Son and believes in Him shall have eternal life…" John 6:40

He knocks… and says, "I am the resurrection and the life. He who believes in Me will live, even though he dies. And everyone who lives and believes in Me will never die." John 11:25

He knocks… and asks, "Do you believe this?" John 11:26

His Authority

A fair and essential question to ask is, "By what authority is this Offer made?" The answer is simple, and the illustration is even simpler. The question brings us back around to He Exists and how important it is that we believe He Exists as the Manual represents. When I was growing up, there were a couple of phrases used commonly by parents. Usually, these phrases were only pulled out after the children had pushed their parents very near the end of their patience. Mom would say, "I brought you into this world, I can take you out!" Dad would say, "As long as you live under my roof, you will follow my rules." Within these desperate phrases are contained some accepted truths. Society has always held that the people responsible (with a little help from God) for giving us life, our parents, have authority over us as a result. When dad wields his phrase, he is saying, "I built this house, it is mine. Because of that, I have the authority to set the rules for anyone who wishes to take advantage of my offer to live here." Again, society has always accepted this premise. And they are not wrong. God not only accepts the premise, He instructs parents to take authority over that which they created. He in no uncertain terms tells parents to guide and discipline, to discourage and praise, to teach their children what is right and what is not. To warn them of actions that lead to death and to show them the safe path. To "Love" their children!

It is this Truth that gives God the Authority. God created… everything. Therefore, everything is His. God brought you and me into the world, and one day we will be taken out. When that day comes, He wants to say, "Well done my good and faithful…" son or daughter. (Matthew 25:21) He sent us **Hope** so that when that day comes, He will not have to say, "Depart from Me; I never knew you…" (Matthew 7:23)

How do we know He has this authority over what He created?

> "You of little faith," Jesus replied, "why are you so afraid?" Then He got up and rebuked the winds and the sea, and it was perfectly calm…Even the winds and the sea obey Him!" Matthew 8:26,27

> "…all that night the LORD drove back the sea with a strong east wind that turned it into dry land. So the waters were divided…" Exodus 14:21

> "Jesus knew what they were thinking and said, 'Why do you harbor evil in your hearts? Which is easier: to say, "Your sins are forgiven," or to say, "Get up and walk?" But so that you may know that the Son of Man has authority on earth to forgive sins…' Then He said to the paralytic, 'Get up, pick up your mat, and go home.' And the man got up and went home." Matthew 9:4-7

"'Lord, by now he stinks,' said Martha, the sister of the dead man. 'It has already been four days.' Jesus replied, <u>'Did I not tell you that if you believed, you would see the glory of God?'</u> After Jesus had said this, He called out in a loud voice, 'Lazarus, come out!' The man who had been dead came out..." John 11:39,40,43,44

Even Satan is only a tenant in this world. He owns nothing. After he chose to deny God, to believe God wasn't exactly who He said He was, God cast him down into the low rent district, "...the outer darkness, where there (is) weeping and gnashing of teeth." (Matthew 25:30) It is this same lie with which Satan, the Adversary, got Adam and Eve and how he gets us. He whispers in our ears, "God's a liar, He didn't create." He says, "God isn't who He says He is. He's holding back on you." So, we question God's authority and, in so doing, reject The Offer. Like children who reach the age of Adulthood and choose for themselves to honor Mom and Dad's teachings or to believe they know better and go a different way, we must choose to honor our Creator or join the Adversary. Today the "outer darkness" is full of those who believed the Adversary and questioned God's Authority.

In Matthew 8:13, Christ said to the centurion, "Go! As you have believed, so will it be done for you." Today, He says the same to you and me. The obvious flip side of that coin is, "As you choose not to believe, nothing can be done for you."

Before we move on, let's take a little closer look at God's Authority and ours. I have made the case that our parents have authority over us in accordance with their "bringing us into this world," but I want to be clear about something. Without God creating us, we would not exist, and without God creating our parents, they would not exist. Therefore, while we are subject to the authority of our parents, our parents are subject to the ultimate Authority of God, as are we. God declares Truth and sets the rules. Our parents must follow those rules in raising and teaching us; otherwise, they will not be "in God's favor."

He Calls to The Lost

"I have gone astray like a lost sheep (sey)…" (Psalms 119:176) "My people have been lost sheep (tsone)…" (Jeremiah 50:6)

Strong's shows that both uses of the word, "sey" and "tsone," refer to "a flock." Sey refers to an individual "member of a flock," such as "a sheep," while tsone refers to the flock as a group, and we all know that the plural of sheep is sheep.

So, who are "The Lost"? In what follows, we will not only discuss who they are but who they are not. In discussing His sheep, God also references two other representative animals: the goat and the wolf. Because it is important to the sheep, lost or found, and to The Offer of Hope, we must look at what He means when He refers to any one of these animals.

First, let's consider sheep. Sheep do not like being alone; they prefer the comfort of being among other sheep, the "flock." This flock mentality serves them well as it makes them less vulnerable to predators (spoiler alert, "Wolves"!). Sheep recognize the voice of their shepherd and come when called.

Goats, on the other hand, prefer to walk alone; they derive no comfort from being part of a group. As a single animal wandering alone, they are easy prey for the wolf. They have no interest in the shepherd's call. They are more concerned with establishing their independence.

That leaves the Wolf. The wolf is a violent animal, happy to travel and hunt in packs. Wolves will fight amongst themselves, to the death if necessary, to establish their dominance in the group. They seek out the sheep who wanders from the flock and the shepherd. Such a sheep is no more than a quick meal to them. If the shepherd is near, they sneak around in the grass, lay low, and wait for the most promising opportunity to strike the lost sheep.

Now that we understand the personalities of these animals, what does God seek to teach us from comparing them to men? First, each will always be what they are. A wolf will always be a wolf, and he will never give up the hunt. A goat will always be a goat, living for themselves, and can't or will never become a sheep. A sheep will always be a sheep, whether they are safe among the flock or "Lost" in the world away from the shepherd.

Again, because of a changing world, let me Re-Set the stage to that which the Manual references. The relationship between the shepherd and his sheep was not what it is today. Back in Jesus' time, the shepherd had a personal relationship with his sheep.

The shepherd walked, talked, and slept with his sheep. He gave each a name so that they would know when he was calling them. So familiar was the shepherd to the sheep that they recognized the sound of his voice to the exclusion of any other. The shepherd was the caregiver, the provider, and the protector of the sheep. If one of his sheep wandered off, he would leave the flock to the safety of their numbers and go out in search of his lost sheep. Concerned for its safety, knowing that wolves abound, he would call it by name to get its attention. He would use the sound of his voice to guide it back to his care. Once found, the lost sheep would be returned to the safety of the flock. The shepherd loved his flock and hated anything that would threaten even one member.

It is the essence of this relationship that makes Hope possible. The Manual says Christ is the Shepherd and believers are His sheep. Christ, Himself says, "I am the good shepherd..." (John 10:11) "My sheep listen to My voice; I know them, and they follow Me." "...because you are not My sheep, you refuse to believe." (John 10:27, 26) Christ continues in John 10:11, "The good shepherd lays down His life for the sheep." Within this statement is **"The Offer."** This is our **"Hope."** "I give them eternal life, and they will never perish. No one can snatch them out of My hand. My Father who has given them to Me is greater than all. No one can snatch them out of My Father's hand. I and the Father are one." (John 10:28-30)

A picture I aquired 30 years ago at a garage sale for $1.50. Who knew
that I would be writing about this today? Answer: He did!

But The Offer is clear. It is for the Believers, for His sheep. It is for those who hear His voice, believe and follow. The Offer is not for the goats, those who do not recognize His voice or His Authority. For it is the character of a goat to be a goat; they will not hear or heed the Shepherd's call. In so doing, they reject The Offer, showing themselves to be unbelievers, goats. A lost sheep may have wandered from following the path of the Shepherd, but they are still His sheep and, when He calls, they will hear. A lost sheep is still a sheep. The only risk to these lost sheep is that they find a wolf before they return to the Shepherd. When the day of our Hope arrives, the Shepherd says this is what will happen: "When the Son of Man comes in His glory, and all the angels with Him, He will sit on His glorious throne. All the nations will be gathered before Him, and He will separate the people one from another, as a shepherd separates the sheep from the goats. He will place the sheep on His right and the goats on His left. Then the King will say to those on His right, 'Come, you who are blessed by My Father, inherit the kingdom prepared for you from the foundation of the world....Then He will say to those on His left, 'Depart from Me, you who are cursed, into the eternal fire prepared for the devil and his angels." (Matthew 25:31-34,41)

But what about those "lost sheep?" "…this is what the Lord GOD says: 'Behold, I Myself will search for My flock and seek them out. As a shepherd looks for his scattered sheep when he is among the flock, so I will look for My flock…I will seek the lost, bring back the strays, bind up the broken, and strengthen the weak." (Ezekiel 34:11,12,16) In other words, "He is our God, and we are the people of His pasture, the sheep under His care." (Psalms 95:7)

Meaning, "I will not leave you as orphans; I will come to you." (John 14:18) **There's your Hope!**

CHAPTER 3

Reservations & Baggage

So, how do we pull all these pieces together? First, we have to understand that the Gift of Salvation offered is not "one and done." 1 Peter 1:9 says, "…now that you are receiving the goal of your faith, the salvation of your souls." The Offer is for **Hope**. Hope for Salvation.

Salvation is not a Gift given that we can put in the closet until the day we face Christ, at which point we pull it off the shelf, blow off the dust and we're good. Salvation is the "Reward" promised by God and accessed through Christ (our **Hope**), but only received by following the Instructions, heeding the Warnings and obeying the Rules. Salvation is the Spiritual Reward for a Physical life of actively walking in Truth, a life of Faith.

I have an illustration that I wrote and like to use. Because I have not come up with a better one, here it is again. When we want to have a nice dinner somewhere, we call and make a reservation. In making the reservation, we have not eaten anything we have merely secured the opportunity to eat at a later date. If between the call and the time reserved we move to another city, break up with our fiancé, lose our job, or any of a thousand things happen to cause us to miss our reservation, then we never receive our meal. Christ, our **Hope**, is **the source** of our Reservation; it is **through** Him that we secure a place at the heavenly table. However, as 1 Peter says, that reservation is for **"the last time."** If between our accepting Christ (our call) and this last time we live a life that does not **obey Him,** we have walked away from our reservation. As 1 Peter also says, **"through Faith"** (an active walk in Truth) we "are protected by God's power" (Grace) "for the salvation that is ready to be revealed in the last time." 1 Thessalonians 4:7,8 confirms: "For God has not called us to impurity, but to holiness. Anyone, then, who rejects this command does not reject man but God, the very One who gives you His Holy Spirit." By rejecting God's commandments, failing to **obey,** we reject God Himself, our reservation, and our place at the table.

The Manual also refers to The Offer as one of inheritance: "…a living hope through the resurrection of Jesus Christ from the dead, and into an inheritance that is imperishable, undefiled, and unfading, reserved in heaven for you, who through faith are shielded by God's power for the salvation that is ready to be revealed in the last time." (1 Peter 1:3-5) When did you ever hear of an inheritance being given when written? I'll help… never. An inheritance is written to be given at a later date. Sometimes, it even comes with rules. Rules that, if broken by the recipient, forfeit their reward.

Let me bend the illustration just a little. I want to move the image from a restaurant to an airport. We all know that you don't typically just walk into an airport, buy a ticket and hop on a plane. We call or go online, find the right flight, and make a reservation to fly at some later date. You get how this compares to the dinner example so I won't go into it. I switched to this example so we could talk about "baggage." If you've ever flown before, you have experienced the hassle of bringing along baggage. There is the baggage you have to send to the cargo hold for transport, the carry-on, and the personal item like a laptop bag. Depending on the airline and the flight, the rules and fees for each are different. In the end, once you meet all the conditions, you are allowed to bring all the baggage you desire. The same is not true of your Reservation for Salvation.

To redeem this Reservation and get through the Gate, you must have no baggage; there are no carry-ons. Many get to the Gate thinking that this rule doesn't mean "no" baggage and they bring along a little personal item. I'm sure they are surprised when security is called and they are escorted away from the gate and handed over to the Adversary who not only allows all their baggage of choice but is all too happy to pile on more. "…nothing unclean will ever enter it, nor anyone who practices an abomination or a lie, but only those whose names are written in the Lamb's book of life." (Revelations 21:27)

Matthew Henry explains:

> "First, Free from such as are openly profane. There are none admitted into heaven who work abominations. In the churches on earth sometimes abominable things are done, solemn ordinances profaned and prostituted to men openly vicious, for worldly ends; but no such abominations can have place in heaven. Secondly, Free from hypocrites, such as make lies... These will creep into the churches of Christ on earth, and may lie concealed there a long time, perhaps all their days; but they cannot intrude into the new Jerusalem, which is wholly reserved for those that are called, and chosen, and faithful, who are all written, not only in the register of the visible church, but in the Lamb's book of life."

It seems obvious. As all that is God is pure, clean and without spot, nothing that isn't, not even a speck, can commune with Him. Sadly, as I researched for this section I found way too many "take what they like" on this issue "and let the rest go." They make the case that "shielded by God's power" means that once you acknowledge Christ, your salvation is set and protected by God. Those who take this position either have the hearing problem we mention in this book or have been led astray by re-definition. The part preceding these words, the part they let go, says, "…reserved in heaven for you, who through faith are…" To be clear, no one dies pure. The best saint to have walked the earth never reached perfection. Those who make the previous argument use this fact to validate their point. Reality check… Truth alert… it doesn't!

"…just as He who called you is holy, so be holy in all you do, for it is written: 'Be holy, because I am holy.' Since you call on a Father who judges each one's work impartially, conduct yourselves in reverent fear during your stay as foreigners… Since you have purified your souls by obedience to the truth." (1 Peter 1:15-17, 22)

Here's the gist of one of the examples I found. (Because this is an all too common scenario, I do not wish to single the "teacher" out. Therefore, I do not directly pull any quotes, only give the accurate gist of the interaction.) A Christian website has a question and answer page. One of the questions submitted is, "Can you die in an act of sin without confessing and still get into Heaven?" The example referenced was a friend who says he is a Christian but gets angry and curses (says a bad word) and says it's OK. First, the questioner doesn't realize how much there is in this seemingly simple question, and sadly neither does the teacher answering. So, let's look at the gist of the answer. Among a litany of other things, 2 Corinthians 1:22 and Ephesians 4:30 are offered as Scriptural support for his answer. These include the fact that we are not saved or kept from being saved by our works. He tells the questioning sheep that we are saved by <u>faith</u> and, referring to the Scripture quotes, that God has sent His Spirit to <u>seal</u> us until the day of redemption. He finishes his counsel with, "What we do or do not do does not affect salvation." He takes the position that all you have to do is "believe" and he quotes some Scriptures.

His definition of belief is one we have already thoroughly shown to be lacking what is required to <u>be</u> a Believer. So, let's move on to Faith. It is obvious that he does not have the correct definition of Faith. The teacher here clearly believes faith is "believing in Christ." As we firmly show in chapter two, it is much more. Re-Set review: **Faith Is** a verb!

Faith Is action! **Faith Is** unyielding confidence! **Faith Is** <u>walking in Truth</u>! It is through this Faith that we show ourselves to be Believers.

So, that's his first error and, as we've shown, not a minor one. Then both of his references are based on the word "seal." Here, again, he seems to have a vocabulary problem. Let's get the quotes in front of us for this discussion: "…placed His seal on us, and put His Spirit in our hearts as a pledge of what is to come." (2 Corinthians 1:22) And from Ephesians: "And do not grieve the Holy Spirit of God, in whom you were sealed for the day of redemption." As I said, his problem lies in misdefining "seal." In the first reference, you only have to look to the end of the quote to fix the problem: "…as a <u>pledge</u> of what is to come." Many translations use some variation of "guarantee" to everything He has promised. You see, "His seal" is referring to God's side of the contract, not ours. He is saying that you can walk in Faith knowing "…it is impossible for God to lie, we who have fled to take hold of the Hope set before us may be strongly encouraged." (Hebrews 6:18) In other words, I am a God of My word, the God of Truth. I will honor my **Offer of Hope**. As stated in Hebrews 7:22, "Because of this oath, Jesus has become the guarantee of a better covenant."

Then there's Ephesians. As is often the case, all you have to do is read the verses around the quote to clear it up: "29 Let no unwholesome talk come out of your mouths, but only what is helpful for building up the one in need and bringing grace to those who listen. <u>30</u> And do not grieve the Holy Spirit of God, in whom you were sealed for the day of redemption. 31 Get rid of all bitterness, rage and anger, outcry and slander, along with every form of malice." Not really sure I need to add much. The quote refers to God's side of the contract. The verses around it and the warning within it refer to ours. The sum up is, God will always honor His side of the deal, but we can always welch on ours.

Returning to Reservations and Baggage. Christ died for our sins because we are not and never could be worthy. It is through paying this price that He bought our reservation. If we accept His offer to hold our reservation we have **Hope**. This reservation does not allow for any baggage. We can choose to walk away from our reservation or try and sneak a little something through the gate with us, but as Henry explained, they will not be admitted into Heaven. If, on the other hand, we follow the Instructions, heed the Warnings, and are obedient to the Rules, when we get to the gate He will say, "Enter, my good and faithful servant."

So, the questions are:

1. What do we actually have to do to make our Reservation, to accept The Offer, to "Secure **Hope**"?

2. What is this "baggage" really?

To sum up the answer to the first question:

1. Confess

2. Die to "Self"

3. Repent

To be understood properly, it is best to look at these three steps together. It used to be said a "Penitent" Belief in Christ is required for Salvation. As just mentioned, Modern Salvation seems to teach that all you have to do is Believe in the Son and you will receive the Father's reward. Many might even throw in, "No, That's Not All... We have to Confess." Some will even manage to add, "We have to Repent." But how many know these two things are not the same, much less, can define the difference? For anyone looking at The Offer, it is vital you understand the answer. To confess is to state a wrong done as wrong... as a sin. To Repent is much more. Strong's says: In Old Testament terms it is to "turn back," in New Testament terms it is to "regret, think differently or to reverse direction." **To Repent is to take action on your Confession and Be Different.** Or, in terms of our illustration, **Confess is to identify our baggage; Repent is to drop that baggage and walk away.** As M'Clure said, "Whoso confesseth and forsaketh his sins shall find mercy." If Repent is to "reverse direction," it seems obvious that the direction to which we have just Confessed must end; we must Die to Self. I think it's fair to say that all baggage – from the little bag we don't think matters to the 500 pounder with wheels and a tow rope – all have the luggage tag "Self" on them somewhere. Isaiah 57:15 says: "...I restore the crushed spirit of the humble and revive the courage of those with repentant hearts." Scripture also says we cannot serve two masters, even (and maybe especially) if that first master is our self. "No one can serve two masters: Either he will hate the one and love the other, or he will be devoted to the one and despise the other." (Matthew 6:24)

Did I just say, "You should hate yourself and love God?"

Well, yes... but again, context. We all have a "Self" that carries the genes of Adam. A Self that listens to the whispers of the Adversary and is tempted to act against God. This Self belongs to the Physical World and would make decisions from that world and not God's world, the Spiritual World. This Self is an idolater. This Self puts something, oftentimes our self, above God. As the Manual says, we cannot serve this master and God. We must hate that Self and be devoted to God. To be painfully clear, the Self of which I speak is not the gift given to us at birth. We are God's creation, we are His temple. As such, we are to respect, honor and dedicate that self to glorifying God "in" this world while remaining firmly "of" the Spiritual World. We must remember God's design: "Let Us make man in Our image, after Our likeness…" (Genesis 1:26) We must live in Pursuit of that original image in which we were created and hate anything that would get in our way. Or, as we have said, we must die to this Self and live for God.

"But," you say, "Christ died to pay the penalty for our sin so we wouldn't have to die." WRONG! Christ died to pay the penalty for our sin so that we might have a way to be "made Righteous." Romans 10:10 "…with your heart you believe and are justified, and with your mouth you confess and are saved." In other words, Christ died so we could be restored to a right relationship with God and enjoy Life Eternal. To receive this blessed gift, we absolutely must die and have a new life, His Life, born anew in us. 2 Thessalonians 2:13 "…God has chosen you from the beginning to be saved by the sanctification (purification) of the Spirit and by faith in the truth." Christ's death served as "propitiation for our sins." (1 John 2:2) We can confess our sins, but, as sons and daughters of Adam, we cannot satisfy what the Law demands. Christ, having been born a Man yet never breaking the Law, fulfilled the Law. Then, unstained, only He was worthy to stand in, or as Hebrews 7:22 says, to be a "surety" for us. (surety- "one who is recognized to answer for another… to pay their debt." Webster's 1828) "God presented Him (Christ) as an atoning sacrifice…" (Romans 3:25), to bring us from "death to life." (John 5:24)

Here's how M'Clure put it:

> "Christ is the end of the ceremonial law, as that law received its fulfillment in him. The ceremonial law was given to the ancient church at Sinai, and consisted of various typical rites & sacrifices…but they were no longer necessary after the promised Saviour had offered up himself, a sacrifice for the sins of men. Christ is the end of the moral law in two respects, first, as he perfectly kept it, and secondly as by his obedience and suffering, a righteousness is finished, by which sinners, whom the law condemns, may be saved." "MANKIND by the guilt of sin forfeited life and fell under the condemnation of the covenant of works. The mercy of God has provided for them the milder dispensation of Grace, by the mediation of our Lord Jesus Christ." "Those who are interested in the righteousness of Jesus Christ are said to be justified." "As the general plan of the redemption of sinners, was an act of Sovran Grace, so also is the application of that redemption to individuals. He hath mercy on whom he will have mercy. And <u>God justly leaves those who reject salvation, to the fatal consequences of their own choice</u>." "The law satisfied by Jesus Christ, and sinners justified by the imputation of his righteousness."

Through His sacrifice we find absolution, we have redemption. Through our deaths, taking up our crosses daily, we are restored to lives lived in absolute, humble surrender and joyful obedience to God as He exists…lives lived in Pursuit of God. We are saved from our denial of Him, from our Rebellion against Him To New Life. "He Himself bore our sins in His body on the tree, so that we might die to sin and live to righteousness." (1 Peter 2:24) The Rebel cannot be cured, cannot be regenerated, cannot be saved. The Rebel cannot walk with Christ. <u>The Rebel Must Die with and for Christ to rise and Live in Christ</u>!

As to the second question, what is "baggage?" The short version: everything to which we must die. Everything that separates us from God. Anything that tarnishes the image in which we were created. Everything and anything that is not good as defined by God in the Manual. The longer version is coming in the chapter "**Instructions, Warnings and The Rules.**"

Inward and Outward

Before going into the "instructions," it is essential that we understand the difference and implication of two words: Inward and Outward. Somewhere along the line, whether by the world's redefining or because the churches have forgotten the difference, these words have been separated from God's Truth and, therefore, neither properly taught nor applied. The first has been reduced to that of tacit compliance with the Secular Morality of the Physical world. The second has been elevated to a role that is not unlike the "wolf in sheep's clothing." Most churches and many of their members take the position that as long as their Outward Acts are that of a sheep, the Inward wolf doesn't matter. Therefore, another Re-Set.

We have talked about how Adam's sin was not the eating of the apple but his accepting the Adversary's lies and choosing to eat the apple. Let me give you another example from my childhood that I think demonstrates the point well. When I was young, cars didn't have "charging ports" they had "cigarette lighters," which, by the way, are exactly the same just missing the lighter insert. This insert was a tiny heating coil that when pushed into the port would heat up. This insert was then removed and touched to the tip of the cigarette to light it. To help you visualize, picture the coil burner on an electric stove shrunk down to the size of a nickel and set inside a short tube with a knob to hold it.

When I was little I was warned as all children were, "That gets very hot... don't touch it!" I know, you see what's coming. Don't jump ahead. My mother did not give this warning to be mean, she gave it to protect me. She understood the limitations of my creation and the danger the lighter represented. Ok, now... One day, a näive and questioning little boy named Scott thought, "How hot can this little thing be?" Then that little boy thought, "One way to find out!" First, that little boy was wrong. He could have believed and trusted the person who brought him into this world. From this error and those questioning whispers two things happened. First, he chose to touch the hot coil. Second, his course having been set, he stuck his finger in the tube. As the wisp of smoke rose, the sizzle commenced and the smell of burnt flesh reached his nose. The boy looked down at his throbbing fingertip to see the exact ring pattern of the tiny burner seared into its tip.

So, where was my error really committed? When I touched the Very Hot lighter? Or was it when I chose to do so? It was at the point I embraced the whispers, adopted them as my own and undeterredly Chose to act on them. I know many would say that until I actually touched the hot coil, I could always change direction. This is where the confusion comes in. That is not true. I could always change direction until the moment I chose "Inwardly" to commit to the idea that I needed to touch it. From that point, the "Outward" act was only evidence of what I had already decided.

So that the weeks of pain I suffered might benefit you, let's look at how this applies to the Firefighter analogy. The Firefighter is there to save you from the burning building. He knows all the dangers that are present and He knows the only safe way out. He calls to you, He offers to save you, and He holds out His hand. When is your fate sealed? Is it at the point when you move toward the Firefighter or toward the flames? Neither! It is the point when you choose "undeterredly" to reject His instruction and His offer. Jumping into the flames is just the Outward evidence of what you had already chosen.

Remember, when we started I told you to keep in mind two worlds, the Spiritual and the Physical. This is one of the most important reasons why. The choice to sin, to act contrary to God's goodness, is Spiritual. The manifestation of sin is Physical. It is the choice to act outside of God's Favor, His Grace, that is the offense. Just as Faith Is the action that demonstrates a belief in God's Truth, sin is the active demonstration of a lack of belief in that same Truth. And it is that lack of belief, that doubt, that accuses God of not being exactly who He says He is. That is the offense!

Let's ask the Firefighter: "You have heard that it was said, 'Do not commit adultery.' But I tell you that anyone who looks at a woman to lust after her has already committed adultery with her in his heart." (Matthew 5:27,28) What Christ says here is that while "sin" might be the Outward (Physical) act against God, the offense is the Inward (Spiritual) choice to disregard His instruction.

> "Who is wise? Let them realize these things. Who is discerning? Let them understand. The ways of the LORD are right; the righteous walk in them, but the rebellious stumble in them." Hosea 14:9

"Whoever heeds instruction will find success, blessed is he who trusts in the LORD. The wise in heart will be called discerning…" Proverbs 16:20,21

The fact that modern churches have forgotten this Truth has caused their teachings to categorize and qualify "acts of sin" over the offense of consciously choosing less than God instructs. We will look closer at "the churches" coming up. By Christ's stated standard, a robber who is committed to taking what is not his but is too afraid of the cost of getting caught to carry it out is by his Spiritual choice guilty of an offense against God. By the same standard, someone who chooses undeterredly to want someone dead but lacks the courage to carry it out has offended God just as much as the one who follows through. The good news is that The Offer says that only one offense is beyond forgiveness… Blasphemy against the Holy Spirit. For the rest, there is **Hope**.

Now, let's look back at our Q&A example. It might be helpful to take a second and look back at the gist of the question. I'll wait……… Got it? OK. There is an assumption made that to curse is a sin. There are a lot of things like this that some churches have added to the list. We will get to the list of Instructions, Warnings, and Rules soon. For now, this raises an interesting question: Can something not specifically on the list be a sin, or, as we just talked about, can it be baggage? For a long time, I held the belief, and still do, that "cursing" or "swearing" in itself is not a sin. Now… keep reading. I, for instance, have met a few people who can only be accurately described by a three-letter word for a donkey. No other word quite gets it. That said, the Manual does not specifically put cursing on the list. No, the Scripture reference above, "unwholesome talk" does not refer to cursing, neither does "obscenity, foolish talk, or crude joking." "Curse words" are words on a list created by man as offensive; they are not on a list in the Manual. But does cursing fall on another list discussed in the Manual? We'll find the answer in a few verses from the Romans section:

> "For none of us lives to himself alone, and none of us dies to himself alone. If we live, we live to the Lord, and if we die, we die to the Lord. So, whether we live or die, we belong to the Lord. For this reason Christ died and returned to life, so that He might be the Lord of both the dead and the living.
>
> So then, each of us will give an account of himself to God.
>
> ...make up your mind not to put any stumbling block or obstacle in your brother's way. I am convinced and fully persuaded in the Lord Jesus that nothing is unclean in itself. But if anyone regards something as unclean, then for him it is unclean. If your brother is distressed by what you eat, you are no longer acting in love. Do not by your eating destroy your brother, for whom Christ died.
>
> Do not destroy the work of God for the sake of food. All food is clean, but it is wrong for a man to let his eating be a stumbling block. It is better not to eat meat or drink wine or to do anything to cause your brother to stumble.
>
> Keep your belief about such matters between yourself and God. Blessed is the one who does not condemn himself by what he approves. But the one who has doubts is condemned if he eats, because his eating is not from faith; and everything that is not from faith is sin." Romans 14:7-9,12-15, 20-23

The Manual is very clear about "stumbling blocks." Here, Paul points out that things that are not on the list can still be sins. If what you do knowingly places a stumbling block in someone else's way or causes you to trip, then it is a sin. In the case to which Paul refers, certain foods were seen to be unclean and, therefore, sinful to eat. Even though the Manual says nothing God makes is unclean, our priority is our fellow sheep, not food. In our questioner's case, God has not declared three-letter or four-letter words bad. However, the world and most sheep, lost or not, have accepted that a Christian does not use this language. So, if I am working alone or with sheep of like mind in the privacy of my garage and I hit my thumb with a hammer and I cry out in pain a four-letter word, I have not sinned. This is because first, and most importantly, cursing is not on the list and secondly, I and those with me do not regard cursing as bad. On the other hand, if I am among those who do believe it is bad, and they question the legitimacy of God because of it... I have sinned.

Quickly, for those who would say... but it says "everything that is not from faith is sin." Yes, but again, context and definition. The context is doubt regarding whether his eating was OK with God. Because he wasn't sure, then his outward act of eating showed an inward choice that he was OK with the possibility of defying God. Again, the definition, it says, "because his eating was not from faith." Meaning, because he questioned the Truth in which he was to walk but ate anyway, his eating was not from Faith (acting in Truth). This is why I waited until after defining sin to discuss this part of the questioner's assumption. He believes that cursing is a sin so, for him it is. Even though his friend believes it isn't, when done in front of him who believes it is, it is sin. This is a necessary context to the questioner's question: if his Christian friend were driving a car, cursed, then hit a tree and died... would he get into heaven? His obvious assumption is what we just discussed: Cursing is a sin. However, as we have just shown, if his friend were not in the car with anyone who believed it was a sin and just before he hit the tree he shouts out in fear a word for a smelly pile, then his words were not a sin.

The sheep's ultimate question was: can a person who has committed any kind of sin but has not taken or had the opportunity to confess and repent of it get into heaven… i.e. can a sinner enter heaven? The premise shows the questioner to be off the mark, namely legalistic and shows the same about the responder just on the other end of the scale. First, common sense tells us it is unlikely that most people have managed to clear themselves from all recent sins at the time of death. While there are exceptions, i.e. Luke 23:40-43, those few who have tried are likely those who took the gamble, ignored the Shepherd's call, and then, when facing death squarely in the face, feared the price. I'm not sure how this works out for those souls. I know that confession and repentance must be born in sincerity and devotion to God's Truth. I wonder whether that can be said of those who appear to be flailing against punishment rather than Truly reaching for God's Love. "… fear involves punishment. The one who fears has not been perfected in love." (1 John 4:18) This is a decision left to God, a decision to determine "condemnation." As we know, while we are instructed to judge according to the Manual, we are forbidden from declaring "final judgment," or condemnation.

Let's address the flawed premises of our Q&A participants: The first takes an Old Testament approach to God. An approach that is achieved through "acts" as well as belief. This is what is meant by the term "legalistic." A legalistic person claiming Christ forgets His teaching to the

Galatians. "Before this faith came, we were held in custody under the law, locked up until faith should be revealed. So the law became our guardian (schoolmaster) to lead us to Christ, that we might be justified by faith. Now that faith has come, we are no longer under a guardian. You are all sons of God through faith in Christ Jesus." (Galatians 3:23-26) The opposite extreme of the legalistic also misses the point and "throws the baby out with the bathwater." It doesn't say that the rules were thrown out or that sin does not bring condemnation. It says that the means of "justification" have changed from ritual sacrifice to Faith in Christ who was the Ultimate Sacrifice. It says that the "law" taught us to follow God's rules and taught us to appeal to God for forgiveness when we fail. Christ brought us the indwelling of the Holy Spirit and taught us that the desire to follow the rules now comes from an inward thirst, not a ritual command. He uses "Faith" five times in those few verses. Remember, Faith is an active walk in God's Truth, a continuous effort to adhere to the rules.

Finally, I just think it's a bad and dangerous habit to try and decide which sins keep you out and which you might get away with. As all sin is the outward act of an inward offense to God, all sin is baggage and no baggage makes it through the gate. This is a gamble I am not willing to take. So, for me, I will not spend any spiritual resources evaluating these issues further. I will live a life in Truth, a life by Faith, a life in hope that I will find God's Grace.

Finally, a short but important warning. As we discussed, the Physical World and the churches who have adopted their morals will declare all kinds of things sinful that are not. I have not just made the case that we should adopt these "sins" defined by the immoral, thereby taking on the Authority of God. Conversely, I was very clear that our discussion was about things above or beyond the clear list described in the Manual. That list includes that we do not add or subtract from God's. God defines what is right and what is wrong, what is an offense to Him and what is not. He adds that anything we do that is the result of doubt in His Truth is a sin. He adds that anything we do that puts a "stumbling block" in the way of our fellow sheep, lost or not, is a sin. Man has no authority to go beyond or be in contrast to God.

CHAPTER 4

Heretics, Hirelings & The Church

You may have noticed that I never quite got around to the Wolves in chapter two. It isn't that I forgot, it's that the wolves deserve a little more attention than the goats. The goats are really only a threat to themselves; the wolves are a threat to the entire flock. "Beware of false prophets. They come to you in sheep's clothing, but inwardly they are ravenous wolves." (Matthew 7:15) Christ says that there will be those who try to enter the flock but are not Believers. These unbelievers pass themselves off as sheep by saying the right things and wearing the wool of the sheep, but they do not hear the Shepherd's voice. These wolves have entered the flock not to join it but to destroy it. "I know that after my departure, savage wolves will come in among you and will not spare the flock. Even from your own number, men will rise up and distort the truth to draw away disciples after them." (Acts 20:29,30) They will come to you saying, "I believe in God but..." They will want the blessing but not the instruction. Like thieves, they will try to steal the Hope Christ offers, avoiding the Narrow Way. "The person who doesn't enter the sheepfold through the gate, but climbs in by some other way, is a thief and a bandit." (John 10:1) "Enter through the narrow gate. For wide is the gate and broad is the way that leads to destruction, and many enter through it. But small is the gate and narrow the way that leads to life, and only a few find it." (Matthew 7:13,14) Remember, Christ is not only the Great Shepherd who stands at the Narrow Gate calling His sheep, but He is also the Gate itself, turning away the goats and the wolves. Christ goes on in Matthew 7: "...by their fruit you will recognize them." (v16) In other words, we are to "judge" what these declaring sheep produce and by this "fruit" identify the tree: sheep or wolf? Christ illustrates in Luke 6:43,44: "No good tree bears bad fruit, nor does a bad tree bear good fruit. For each tree is known by its own fruit. Indeed, people do not gather figs from thornbushes, or grapes from brambles." Later, we will talk about what Christ says to do with these "bad trees." A wolf may be able to disguise its appearance but, hard as it may try to hide, it cannot change its heart. A wolf will still be a wolf. "For out of the overflow of the heart, the mouth speaks." (Luke 6:45)

Sometimes these wolves don't just wear sheep's clothing, they don the robes of a shepherd. "Woe to the shepherds who destroy and scatter the sheep of My pasture!' declares the LORD...I will bestow punishment on you for the evil you have done." (Jeremiah 23:1,2) "Tell those who prophesy out of their own imagination: 'Hear the word of the LORD! This is what the Lord GOD says: Woe to the foolish prophets who follow their own spirit, yet have seen nothing...Because of your false words and lying visions, I am against you." (Ezekiel 13:2,3,8) "Now there were also false prophets among the people, just as there will be false teachers among you...because of them the way of truth will be defamed. In their greed, these false teachers will exploit you with deceptive words...These men are like irrational animals, creatures of instinct, born to be captured and destroyed...They have left the straight way and wandered off to follow the way of Balaam son of Beor, who loved the wages of wickedness." (2 Peter 2:1-3,12,15)

The point here is this, whether it was the scribes and Pharisees, the Nicolaitans, or the people at the local church, there will always be those who work to steal or at least make you forget your Hope. The many packs of wolves running around this world are easy to identify and, therefore, are not actually the greatest threat. It is the cunning wolf who adorns itself with the best sheepskin and slips in among the flock. Worse yet, it is the wolf that passes himself off so well as a sheep that he is promoted and accepted as a shepherd. From this position of authority, he can decimate a flock, forever robbing some of their Hope. In the pages to come, we will go into all the ways you can identify these threats and guard your Hope against them. Above, we gave the most important one: "by their fruit you will know them." But, in order to identify the fruit, you must have a reference. This reference is the Manual given to us by God, and coming up we discuss thoroughly what it is and what it is not. The Truth you can have Faith in here is this: The Great Shepherd has not left you unprotected. He offers you the Holy Ghost to "teach you all things." He knows your name and your Hope is secure.

Beware the "Nicolaitans"

Tozer said, "Heresy is not so much rejecting as selecting. The heretic simply selects the parts of the Scripture he wants to emphasize and lets the rest go." Was he right? If he was, is it really that bad? Enter the Nicolaitans. It's likely you've never heard of them or, if you did, it was such a brief reference in a Scripture reading that they passed right by you. I'll start with those Scriptures and then introduce you to the Nicolaitans. Christ said of them in Revelation 2:6, "But you have this to your credit: You hate the works of the Nicolaitans, which I also hate." Christ references them again in Revelation 2:15,16, "…some of you also hold to the teaching of the Nicolaitans. Therefore repent! Otherwise I will come to you shortly and wage war against them with the sword of My mouth." And that's it. So why make such a big deal out of such an obscure reference? Because of what these references are attached to and who the Nicolaitans were. Most Bible scholars agree that the Nicolaitans were followers of Nicolas. Who was Nicolas?

> "So the Twelve summoned all the disciples and said, "It is unacceptable for us to neglect the word of God in order to wait on tables. Therefore, brothers, select from among you seven men confirmed to be full of the Spirit and wisdom.

We will appoint this responsibility to them and devote ourselves to prayer and the ministry of the word."

This proposal pleased the whole group. They chose Stephen, a man full of faith and of the Holy Spirit, as well as Philip, Prochorus, Nicanor, Timon, Parmenas, and Nicolas from Antioch, a convert to Judaism. They presented these seven to the apostles, who prayed and laid their hands on them.

So the word of God continued to spread. The number of disciples in Jerusalem grew rapidly, and a great number of priests became obedient to the faith." Acts 6:2-7

Nicolas was a pagan who "converted to Judaism," then a Jew who converted to Christianity. This path is important because even though he was chosen to shepherd others and to teach the word of God, he became a warning to the churches. These quotes are taken from John's letters to the churches where he writes, "…blessed are those who hear and obey what is written…" (Revelation 1:3) What was written? "On the Lord's day I was in the Spirit, and I heard behind me a loud voice like a trumpet, saying, 'Write in a scroll what you see and send it to the seven churches: to Ephesus, Smyrna, Pergamum, Thyatira, Sardis, Philadelphia, and Laodicea.'" (Revelation 1:10,11) The first reference was written to the church in Ephesus. Christ commends the church for not "…tolerating those who are evil, and you have tested and exposed as liars those who falsely claim to be apostles." (Revelation 2:2) He chastises their failings and then returns to say, "But you have this to your credit: You hate the works of the Nicolaitans, which I also hate." (Revelation 2:6) He then brings them up again in His letter to the church in Pergamum saying, "But I have a few things against you, because some of you hold to the teaching of Balaam, who taught Balak to place a stumbling block before the Israelites so they would eat food sacrificed to idols and commit sexual immorality. In the same way, some of you also hold to the teaching of the Nicolaitans. Therefore repent!" (Revelation 2:14-16) Christ compares the Nicolaitans to Balaam who is recorded in the book of Numbers: "…through the counsel of Balaam, (taught the sons of Israel) to turn unfaithfully against the LORD at Peor, so that the plague struck the congregation of the LORD." (Numbers 31:16)

Balaam told Balak how to get the Israelites to compromise their Faith. Nicolas did the same. The Nicolaitans may have been the first Christian based cult. You see, Nicolas never completely let go of his past and decided to edit Christ's teachings. He "let go" of the parts he didn't like. Nicolas was a Heretic. Nicolas and his followers took God's Authority on themselves and re-wrote His instructions.

Nicolas was more than just a heretic. Because he was charged with being a shepherd and he used that position to lead people astray, to put a "stumbling block" in their way, he was a "false prophet." Peter, who would have known of the Nicolaitans' heresy warned, "Now there were false prophets also among the people, even as there shall be false teachers among you, who privily shall bring in damnable heresies, even denying the Lord that bought them, and bring upon themselves swift destruction." (2 Peter 2:1) Paul also warned about people like Nicolas: "Avoid a man who is a heretic after the first and second admonitions, and be aware that he who is such is perverse and a sinner and is self-condemned." (Titus 3:10,11)

Tozer is right, but what does the Manual say heresy is? From Deuteronomy: "You must not add to or subtract from what I command you…" (4:2) and "See that you do everything I command you; do not add to it or subtract from it." (12:32) From Revelation: "And if anyone takes away from the words of this book of prophecy, God will take away his share in the tree of life and in the holy city, which are described in this book." (22:19) and "…If anyone adds to them, God will add to him the plagues described in this book." (22:18) Finally, what does John say about people who edit Scripture like the Nicolaitans? "Anyone who runs ahead without remaining in the teaching of Christ does not have God. Whoever remains in His teaching has both the Father and the Son. If anyone comes to you but does not bring this teaching, do not receive him into your home or even greet him. (some translations use "welcome") Whoever greets such a person shares in his evil deeds." (2 John 1:9-11) Henry said of heresy: "How great an evil real heresy is… greatly to be taken heed of by all." He also said, "Such a one is subverted or perverted—a metaphor from a building so ruined as to render it difficult if not impossible to repair and raise it up again. Real heretics have seldom been recovered to the true faith: not so much defect of judgment, as perverseness of the will, being in the case, through pride, or ambition, or self-willedness, or covetousness, or such like corruption, which therefore must be taken heed of." Henry's solution: "Be humble, love the Truth and practice it, and damning heresy will be escaped."

I think we've packed enough references in this section to prove it undeniable that God reserves a sovereign Authority over His creation, and any person who presumes to take that authority on themselves, like Balaam, will not like the results. Whether a shepherd like Nicolas or just a follower, the fate is the same… **Hope** is lost.

"The Church"

First, because these days we have confused "The Church" with the churches, I want to take a minute to Re-Set our understanding to match the Manual. Strong refers to The Church as a Community of Christians. I like how it is described in the second chapter of Acts: "Fellowship of Believers." Acts 2 describes the events around Peter speaking to the crowd on the Day of Pentecost. Verse 41 says, "…about three thousand were <u>added to the believers</u> that day." Verse 42 goes on to say, "<u>They devoted themselves to the apostles' teaching</u> and to the fellowship, to the breaking of bread and to prayer." Verses 44 and 46 further clarify: "<u>All the believers</u> were together <u>and had everything in common… With one accord</u> they continued to meet daily in the temple courts and to break bread from house to house…" and that they did so with "sincerity of heart." Finally, verse 47 says, "<u>the Lord added</u> to their number daily <u>those who were being saved</u>." This is all the Biblical reference we need. In Matthew 16:18 Christ says, "I tell you that you are Peter, and on this rock I will build My church, and the gates of Hades will not prevail against it."

On the day of Pentecost, Peter and the Apostles started "The Church." This Church is referred to in the Manual as the "Bride" of Christ. So, while a bride may be seen in many different locations, she is still just one bride. This simple Truth, while commonly understood, has been forgotten in practice. Churches will claim legitimacy based on all sorts of criteria from Pedigree to Population, but, as I will show in subsequent chapters, far too many fail to meet the basic requirements of The Church Christ endorsed. Let's look at those requirements:

They were <u>All Believers</u>

They had <u>Everything in Common</u>

They were of <u>One Accord</u>

They <u>Devoted</u> Themselves to the <u>Apostles' Teaching</u>

They were <u>Saved</u>

The Church is the "Sheepfold" referenced previously. So, what is a sheepfold? Webster's 1828 says that it is "a place where sheep are collected." The Greek word is "aulē," which means Palace or Mansion courtyard. I like the image from the old Westerns of the Mexican villa surrounded by tall adobe walls with one small gate through which you gained access to the yard and the house. For those who don't know what I'm talking about, think about the shots of celebrity mansions completely surrounded by brick walls with the metal gate at the drive as the only way in. In the Western, the walls kept out bandits and dangerous predators like wolves; in Hollywood, paparazzi. You get the idea. The sheepfold is the place where Christ, The Great Shepherd, gathers His sheep. The Manual states that the only way into that sheepfold is through the "Narrow Gate." The only way through the Gate is Christ. It has already been made quite clear that Christ only lets His sheep through the Gate. No goats and No wolves! I know all this seems rather obvious, but sadly this is not the standard followed by most churches today.

Since common sense isn't all that common, let's look at the Manual for further instruction.

"Behold, <u>I am sending you out</u> like sheep among wolves…"
Matthew 10:16

"The harvest is plentiful, but the workers are few. Ask the Lord of the harvest, therefore, to send out workers into His harvest." Matthew 9:37,38

"These twelve Jesus sent out… Go rather to the lost sheep of Israel. As you go, preach this message: 'The kingdom of heaven is near.'" Matthew 10:5-7

"Not everyone who says to Me, 'Lord, Lord,' will enter the kingdom of heaven, but only he who does the will of My Father in heaven." Matthew 7:21

For those who would read these quotes and say these lost sheep were Israel: "I have other sheep that are not of this fold. I must bring them in as well, and they will listen to My voice. Then there will be one flock and one shepherd." (John 10:16) The "sheep that are not of this fold" are all those who hear the Shepherd's voice but are not Jews.

And the Big One, **"The Great Commission"**: "Go into all the world and preach the gospel to every creature. Whoever believes and is baptized will be saved, but whoever does not believe will be condemned." (Mark 16:15,16) "Then Jesus came to them and said, "All authority in heaven and on earth has been given to Me. Therefore, go and make disciples of all nations, baptizing them in the name of the Father, and of the Son, and of the Holy Spirit, and teaching them to obey all that I have commanded you. And surely I am with you always, to the very end of the age." (Matthew 28:18-20)

Finally, how did Christ handle His flock?

"Early in the morning, while it was still dark, Jesus got up and slipped out to a solitary place to pray." Mark 1:35

"As Jesus was going up to Jerusalem, <u>He took the twelve disciples aside</u> and said…" Matthew 20:17

"<u>Jesus called them aside</u> and said…" Matthew 20:25

"<u>After Jesus had finished instructing His twelve disciples</u>, He went on from there to teach and preach in the nearby towns." Matthew 11:1

"<u>Jesus took</u> with Him Peter, James, and John the brother of James, <u>and led them up</u> a high mountain <u>by themselves</u>. There He was transfigured before them." Matthew 17:1,2

"Afterward <u>the disciples came to Jesus privately</u> and asked, "Why couldn't we drive it out?" Matthew 17:19

"He did not say anything to them without a parable. But <u>privately He explained everything to His own disciples</u>." Mark 4:34

When it was time to feed, rest and instruct His flock, Christ took them into His fold away from the crowds, the goats and the wolves. When Christ Himself Shepherded the flock, All were not welcome in His fold… only the sheep!

Anyway, the sum up is this. The Church is a place where the sheep are to be nourished, rejuvenated and kept safe from wolves. The members of The Church being strong and well-fed are to be sent out "among (the) wolves" to look for and minister to the "Lost Sheep." These members are to return to the safety of the fold to rest and recharge under the care of the Shepherd before being sent back out on the search. They are not to bring the goats into the fold to steal from the flock. Nor are they to bring in the wolf to endanger the flock. Again, common sense; what shepherd would bring a goat in to eat all the sheep's food, fight with the sheep and just be a general nuisance? Answer – none! What shepherd would even consider bringing any predator into the safety of the fold, all but guaranteeing harm to the flock? Again, none!

Christ went out to find the sheep. Christ sent the Apostles out... The Apostles sent the disciples out… Yet, most, if not all, churches today market to the world, welcoming all, sheep, goat and wolf alike. They do not follow the standard set by the first Church or by Christ. As Havner crossed the country bringing Revival he affirmed this Truth: "Our Lord sent His disciples out as sheep among wolves; now the wolves are being invited into the sheepfold." When Christ got done calling to the sheep, He took the Apostles into private to teach, discipline and support. He then sent them back out to find more Lost Sheep and "add" them to the Fold. The point? The Church cannot be identified by simply having "church" in their name or on their building. Tax-exempt is an agreement between them and Uncle Sam, not them and God. They are not a church because of their "spiritual lineage," but because of their obedience to The Shepherd. For the sheep looking for a Fold, I say this: Do your homework. Don't be intimidated or sold. Read every bit of their stated Doctrine and compare it to the Manual. If they have "added or subtracted from" it, they are not Christ's shepherds, they are Heretics in sheep's clothing… Move On!

To be clear, everyone attending one of these churches are not either wolves or goats; some are lost sheep unaware they have been lured in. These sheep are not beyond the sound of His call. It has been my experience, however, that a lot of those in these churches tend to be self-focused goats. Also, as the pastor of a church, you take on a role of responsibility to the flock. Therefore, ignorance is not an excuse. These people are Hirelings (Hired Hands) or, as Tozer describes them, "racketeers," in for the con or the career, not the Calling. These are also described by Christ in John 10. Christ says, "The hired hand is not the shepherd…" (verse 12) Equally bad is the wolf who has deceived the flock until given this position of authority so that he is not only a threat to the current flock but can prey on any lost sheep that find their way to the door. To these false prophets, teachers, and pastors, God also has a word: "Woe to the shepherds who destroy and scatter the sheep of My pasture!" declares the LORD." (Jeremiah 23:1) We will come back to these and their folds of broad gates later.

The Sanctuary

In Hebrew, miqdâsh: a consecrated place or asylum, a holy place. In Greek, hagion: a sacred spot or holy place. Referencing Psalm 73:17, Webster's 1828 dictionary puts it like this: "A house consecrated to the worship of God; a place where divine service is performed."

We've shown that a church is to be part of The Church and, as such, must abide by the Manual's instruction on what that means. This has provided us with the foundation of what a church is, but what is built on that foundation is much more. "Give unto the LORD the glory due unto His name." (1 Chronicles 16:29) This is really it. Where might we come together as "one flock" to do this? "A house Consecrated to the Worship of God." It is Worship that turns a church into a Sanctuary. The lack of True Worship is the fruit that reveals the church to be a "Bad Tree."

If we are going to judge this fruit, we better get to know what it looks like, smells like and tastes like. To define Worship, Webster's 1828 uses descriptions like "reverence with supreme respect" and "honor with extravagant love and extreme submission." The Greek and Hebrew words for Worship include these definitions: "Fall down, Humbly beseech, Prostrate oneself in homage, Revere, Adore, Serve, to Bow or Crouch down." While all these ingredients are important, in studying the Truth about Worship, one stood out to me: "Humbly Beseech." If we are ever to Truly Worship, we must understand this.

Isaiah 57:15 says: "The high and lofty one who lives in eternity, the Holy One, says this: 'I live in the high and holy place with those whose spirits are contrite and humble...'" Here Isaiah pairs humble with contrite, so I wanted to look a little deeper at this. The Hebrew word used is dâkâ', which according to Strong's means, "to crumble; transitively to bruise (literally or figuratively): – beat to pieces, break (in pieces), bruise, contrite, crush, destroy, humble." So, that's contrite. How does the Manual use humble? Well, there are nearly a half-dozen words used for humble, their definitions include: "Abase self, Chasten self, Submit self, bring down into Subjection, Bring low, Cast down, to Humble self." (Well, we know a goat can't worship!) Isaiah goes on to say, "...I restore the crushed spirit of the humble and revive the courage of those with repentant hearts." Proverbs 16 clarifies, "All the ways of a man are clean in his own sight, But the LORD weighs the motives. Everyone who is proud in heart is an abomination to the LORD... The mind of man plans his way, But the LORD directs his steps. Pride goes before destruction, and a haughty spirit before a fall. It is better to be humble in spirit with the lowly than to divide the spoil with the proud. Those who listen to instruction will be joyful; those who trust the LORD will be happy." (Proverbs 16:2,5,9,18-20) Verse 18 is usually quoted as "Pride goes before a fall," leaving "haughty" out and, thereby, leaving out an important distinction. Haughty deepens the word pride. Webster's 1828 provides that clarification. It defines haughty not just as pride but "excessive pride," and not just excessive pride but "pride mingled with contempt." Haughty is not just pride but "pride and disdain." In short, an **arrogant spirit goes before a fall**, but a Humble spirit will be joyful and happy. (So much for the wolves.)

It is clear, that to be "**Humble and Contrite**" we must crush our ways and **submit** ourselves to God's ways. We are to fall down, to bring our **self** low and to destroy our **self**. It is only in this state that God can "restore the crushed spirit" and "revive the courage of our repentant hearts." As Isaiah says in 57:12: "He will expose your righteousness and your works, and they will not benefit you." This may sound familiar: In Truth, By Faith, Through Grace. It's saying God will expose the worthlessness of our works and self-righteousness and of our idols. And when we cry out we will see that "all is meaningless except God." But He also says we have a "choice" we can "take refuge in Him." We can choose **Hope**.

So, you choose Hope, now what? How do you find the authentic sheep, the secure fold, the place of Worship, The Sanctuary? I don't know what I would have done if you hadn't asked! Those who are not "contrite and humble," who have not Truly chosen Hope, look like this: "All their deeds are done for men to see...They love the places of honor at banquets, the chief seats in the synagogues, the greetings in the marketplaces..." (Matthew 23:5,6; 7:5) Christ teaches that we need to be this: "Jesus called a little child to stand among them. 'Truly I tell you,' He said, 'unless you change and become like little children, you will never enter the kingdom of heaven. Therefore, whoever humbles himself like this little child is the greatest in the kingdom of heaven. And whoever welcomes a little child like this in My name welcomes Me." (Matthew 18:2-5)

We've all thought of this lesson from Christ and contemplated the innocence of a child, but it's more than that. Children are not arrogant or **self**-sufficient. They don't know what they "know" so they **submit** themselves to the knowledge, guidance, and safety of their parents. They are blank slates, open and eager to learn, **grateful** for all their parents have to offer. <u>You might even say they "worship" them</u>. But, as Matthew 23 continues, those who are not His sheep are not like children, they "exalt themselves," they are "blind guides," even though verse 12 says, "whoever exalts himself will be humbled, and whoever humbles himself will be exalted." They view themselves as "gifts on the altar," "gold on the temple," even though verses 16,18-22 say: "Woe to you, blind guides! You say, 'If anyone swears by the temple, it means nothing; but if anyone swears by the gold of the temple, he is bound by his oath.' You say, 'If anyone swears by the altar, it means nothing; but if anyone swears by the gift on it, he is bound by his oath.' You blind men! Which is greater: the gift, or the altar that makes it sacred? So then, he who swears by the altar swears by it and by everything on it. And he who swears by the temple swears by it and by the One who dwells in it. And he who swears by heaven swears by God's throne and by the One who sits on it." They are like cups that they clean and polish on the outside but on the inside are "full of greed and self-indulgence." Even though verses 26 and 28 say: "First clean the inside of the cup and dish, so that the outside may become clean as well. In the same way, you appear to be righteous on the outside, but on the inside you are full of hypocrisy and wickedness."

How do we avoid this pride, this haughtiness, this Arrogance? Thank goodness for the James section of the Manual! In referencing Proverbs 3:34: "God opposes the proud, but gives Grace to the humble," James says, "Submit yourselves, then, to God. Resist the devil, and he will flee from you. Draw near to God, and He will draw near to you. Cleanse your hands, you sinners, and purify your hearts, you double-minded. Grieve, mourn, and weep. Turn your laughter to mourning, and your joy to gloom. Humble yourselves before the Lord, and He will exalt you." (James 4:7-10) In other words, we must **Humbly beseech**, we must **subdue** and **submit self** to the Lord. Lady Julian put it like this: "Beseeching is a true, gracious, lasting will of the soul, one with and fastened into the will of our Lord by the sweet inward work of the Holy Ghost." Only then can we truly Worship. Only from there, only with these sheep, can a church become a Sanctuary.

One more question. Can we possibly Worship God in the church if we are not living a life of Truth? Jesus told the Samaritan woman this: "But a time is coming and has now come when the true worshipers will worship the Father in spirit and in truth, for the Father is seeking such as these to worship Him. God is Spirit, and His worshipers must worship Him in spirit and in truth." (John 4:23,24) Refresher, what is "Truth"? "I worship the God of our fathers according to the Way, which they call a sect. I believe everything that is laid down by the Law and written in the Prophets." (Acts 24:14) And "For it is written: 'Worship the Lord your God and serve Him only.'" (Matthew 4:10) What does this Worship look like? How do we serve Him only? Can our worship turn to other things and what happens if it does? Deuteronomy 30:15-18 answers these questions: "See, I have set before you today life and prosperity, and death and adversity; in that I command you today to love the LORD your God, to walk in His ways and to keep His commandments and His statutes and His judgments, that you may live and multiply, and that the LORD your God may bless you... But if your heart turns away and you will not listen (obey), but are drawn away and worship other gods and serve them, I declare to you today that you shall surely perish..." In other words, Truth Is the Word declared by God and documented in the Scriptures by the prophets under the "Divine Influence" of God. Worship requires Humble submission to His Authority and a sincere commitment to follow the uncorrupted Manual.

So, how do I know that a church without such a Sanctuary is not a Fold Shepherded by Christ? "So as I live,' declares the Lord GOD, 'surely, because you have defiled My Sanctuary with all your detestable idols and with all your abominations, therefore I will also withdraw, and My eye will have no pity and I will not spare.'" (Ezekiel 5:11)

One last thought. If we as sheep view ourselves as Sanctuaries living lives that put "self" where it belongs, if we make our hearts "Sacred Places," if we live lives of "Reverence" to God, The Shepherd, and The Spirit, then each of us will walk into that church as "a House Consecrated to the Worship of God." As such, we will recognize our fellow sheep. We will reject a fold where goats, wolves and hirelings are present. Our cups will be cleaned from the inside out and the world will see our Shepherd in us. They too will see **Hope**.

CHAPTER 5

Simon Says & The Manual

In his article "No Saviorhood Without Lordship," Tozer said, "Mankind appears to have a positive genius for twisting truth until it ceases to be truth and becomes downright falsehood." As pointed out in the Truth Is section, Truth is defined by God and there is only one Truth in every situation. While Tozer's point is valid, we must remember that even the slightest alteration to Truth is taking on an authority that is not ours. Christ is very clear to whom this authority belonged: "I have much to say about you and much to judge. But the One who sent Me is truthful, and what I have heard from Him, I tell the world." (John 8:26) Christ follows this declaration with: "…I am the way and the truth and the life. No one comes to the Father except through Me." (John 14:6) Christ states unquestionably that it is God who has the Authority to define Truth, to make The Offer, and to set the Rules.

Let me give you M'Clure's full quote: "By sincere repentance, a cordial faith in Jesus Christ and persevering obedience to his gospel, men are to secure a good Hope of eternal life." As usual, I found it helpful to define a few words with the help of Webster's 1828:

> **Cordial:** of or relating to the heart - vital, sincerely or deeply felt, not hypocritical.

> **Sincere:** Pure, being in reality what it appears to be; not feigned; not simulated; not assumed or said for the sake of appearance; real; not hypocritical or pretended.

> **Persevering:** Constant in the execution of a purpose or enterprise.

With these definitions in hand, let me expand M'Clure's statement: "By Pure and Truthful repentance, a Deep, Heartfelt walk in the Truth of Jesus Christ, and Constant obedience to His Gospel, men are to secure a good Hope of eternal life." It's all there. Let's dig in.

Most people are either a fan of some sort of sport or have sat through the experience of watching a game with someone who is. First, we'll set the foundation of the experience. Someone created the game. In so doing, the creator declared rules, boundaries, and penalties for those playing. These regulations are made known to every player, coach, and fan and accepted by all. Now, as the game is played, if any of these rules are broken and the people in charge of enforcement fail to enforce them, the rant commences. The fan screams, "They know the rules, they broke them, they should be penalized!" perhaps with more colorful language. This is true across the board, with any sport, and any fan. They expect the game to be played by the rules set by the creator. The players expect the same. You don't think so? I have never watched a game where some player believes they were fouled that they didn't start jumping and pointing fingers. They expect the ref to enforce the creator's rules. Nobody, player or fan, fights for the rules to be thrown out. We all accept the notion that everything in life comes with rules and if we want to play the game, we need to respect them.

On to Simon Says. Most of us probably remember the game and still can't quite rub our belly and pat our head at the same time. But who is this Simon? And who made him boss? Interestingly, the game started in the century before Christ. Then called "Cicero says," it was named after Marcus Tullius Cicero. Cicero, if you don't already know, was a man not to be trifled with. Well, until Mark Anthony came along and relieved him of his head! Still, until that weight was lifted off his shoulders, if Cicero said it, you did it. In other words, if "Cicero says, 'Do this,'" you do it! But the question was, who is this Simon? This Simon was Simon De Montfort of 13th century France. This Simon had such authority that when he said, "Put King Henry III in prison," King Henry III got put in prison. When Simon said, "Replace the King with a democratic parliament," a parliament it was. So, "Cicero says" gave way to, "Simon says do this," and when, "Simon says," no one questions.

So, why the history lesson? Because Simon Says is not just a game. Simon Says is based on real-life experience and is representative of something very important. Simon Says shows that before Christ's birth, we not only recognized that some (usually the powerful) have the authority to instruct others, we trained our children to accept this premise. While the world 2000 years later has become a lot less respectful, this rule still holds true in every person's life. For at least some period, we acknowledge our parent's authority to say, "Mom says," and have it obeyed. We go to school and accept the authority of the "Teacher Says" and we listen. We accept the Simon Says premise continuously in our daily lives from birth to death. "The Boss Says," and we act. "Uncle Sam Says," and we pay our taxes. We even accept this authority by proxy. When the State puts up a sign and the "Sign Says" stop, we stop. When the "Alarm Clock Says, 'Rise and shine,'" we get up. We accept instruction from all sorts of places. When our "Body Says, 'I'm tired. Lie down,'" we go to bed. When the "Weatherman Says, 'Take an umbrella...'" well, OK, we might just be hedging our bets with that one! But you get the point. On an average day, every one of us acknowledges authority over us in multiple ways and we accept it and comply. We not only accept it, we expect it.

So, let me ask you and think hard: from the short list just mentioned or from scouring your own life, who do you owe? Who on that list can truly Create? Who created you? Who do you know commands authority over the sun and the stars? Who can raise the oceans and part the seas on demand? Who has the power of God? Who died for you? Who took the keys to Hell for you? Who holds out His hand for you? **Who offers you Hope?** Based on these answers I ask: Why is God the One we question? Why, when "God Says," do we say, "Are you sure?" Why, when "God Says," do we say, "but I..."? Why, when "God Says" do we say, "Sorry, that's too hard"? Who do you treat like Mark Anthony when they are only Cicero? Who do we ignorantly give authority over God? What or who are the idols in our lives? Why, when "God Says," do we say, "But Pastor says"? When "God Says, 'Sin is sin and here's the list,'" why do we say, "but the world has its own list and it's not nearly as long"? When "God Says, 'Get up and walk,'" why do we say, "But I don't want to"? When "God Says, 'Here's My Son,'" why do we say, "I'll think about it"? When "God Says, 'He that believes in Him will have eternal life,'" why do we say, "OK, but when You say 'believe...'"? When "God Says" this Gift of Eternal Life comes with some rules why do we say, "RULES??????"?

When the "World Says, 'You can drive, but there are rules,'" we say, "OK." When the "World Says, 'You can drink, but there are rules,'" we say, "OK." When the "World Says, 'You can be a lawyer or a doctor, but you must study, know and practice these books,'" we say, "OK." There is very little that the "World Says" we can do that does not have rules attached that we must accept. Why then, when "God Says" there are rules, are we outraged?

"Constant Obedience" is not just something that fell out of M'Clure's mouth one day. This is well documented in the Manual. First, Paul reminds us that the Manual, The Offer, and the rules for The Offer included in the Manual are all given by God in His Authority, not man's. "For I certify to you, brothers, that the gospel I preached is not devised by man. I did not receive it from any man, nor was I taught it; rather, I received it by revelation from Jesus Christ." (Galatians 1:11,12) I want to take a second and point you back to our discussion in chapter 1. God, under His Authority as our Creator, gives us a Manual for the proper, safe, and beneficial operation of our Gift... Life. This Manual is not a bunch of "burdensome" negatives but a list of instructions and positive warnings. This Manual contains do's to get the most out of our Gift. It contains don'ts to protect our enjoyment and ultimately the longevity (eternity) of our Gift. It contains warnings about how to avoid the fire. It warns us of what we can do to get expelled from the game. Finally, it offers us an extended warranty, it offers Hope, and it gives us a summary of the innumerable rewards of embracing this Hope and following the rules.

One of the toughest things we must do to understand The Offer and embrace the Manual is to withstand the barrage of lies from the Adversary. Sadly, the hardest attacks often come from those close to us and far too often the "Christian" (Nicolaitan) next to us. The Manual explains this too: "The god (small g) of this age has blinded the minds of unbelievers so they cannot see the light (enlightenment) of the gospel of the glory of Christ, who is the image of God." (2 Corinthians 4:4) Those who serve the Adversary, who wish to steal your Hope, deny the Truth. They are perishing and want to take you with them: "And even if our gospel is hidden, it is hidden only to those who are perishing." (2 Corinthians 4:3) So, as Paul and Peter both say, what they cannot understand they "corrupt and distort." You see, the Adversary understands something most Modern Christians and the World seem to miss. He doesn't have to get us to choose him; he just has to get us to deny God. Not even outright, just a little. Adam "walked with God" in the garden. He didn't deny His existence. He simply listened to the whispers of the Adversary and doubted God was exactly who He said He was. That's it! This is what the Israelites did that cost them entry into paradise. This is what the Nicolaitans did that brought them eternal disgrace and their brief mention as a warning to avoid the fire.

Paul says that unbelievers are "blinded" to the Truth. Well, you would have to be blind, deaf, and dumb to miss God's offer. But don't take it from me; **take it from a blind man**. The Pharisees said this after Christ healed the blind man: "We do not know where this man is from." The blind man replied:

> "'That is remarkable indeed!' the man said. 'You do not know where He is from, and yet He opened my eyes. We know that God does not listen to sinners, but He does listen to the one who worships Him and does His will. Never before has anyone heard of opening the eyes of a man born blind. If this man were not from God, He could do no such thing.'" John 9:29-33

The Manual

"The Scriptures afford more light than the brightest human authors. In them the ignorant may learn all requisite knowledge, and the most knowing may learn to discern their ignorance." Robert Boyle. Understanding what the Bible is and what it isn't is key to understanding The Offer, Hope itself, and our role in it. So, let's start with what the Bible isn't. The Adversary has successfully hidden The Offer by getting the world to look for what he knows isn't there. And because too many Christians today lack true Faith, they either go along or get sucked into defending something God never intended. As I pointed out in the beginning, we have allowed the world to re-define our vocabulary and even the definitions of that vocabulary. We allow the world to set the discussion parameters as well as our positions in those discussions and then we proceed to defend the positions we were given. Because we allow the world as it degrades to rewrite the meaning of the words we use, we lose the ability to communicate God, His morality, His character, and His Offer of Hope to that world. But we have taken it one step further. We have allowed this same degrading, unbelieving world to define the Scriptures and to put words in God's mouth. This effectively puts the world above God, allowing it to assume His Authority. This is why Modern Christianity is failing. They wander in the darkness without the Light.

Even in Boyle's day this problem already existed. In his dismantling of these positions he said:

> "…the objections I meet with against the Scriptures are a mournful evidence that the true God himself is not free from the aspersions of his presumptuous creatures, who arrogantly venture to quarrel with his revelations, as well as with his providence; and we have to grieve, that men are to be found who express no more reverence for what He hath dictated, than for what he hath dispensed."

First, the world declares, and it is taught from too many pulpits, that the Bible is The Autobiography of God. In its arrogance, the world has demanded that the Scriptures explain God's existence and His power. They require God to justify His actions, and the church, with its collective tail between its legs, says, "Maybe they have a point." Christianity today sits quietly by while the Adversary, through his proxies both in the church and out, issues a decree that God explains how He is God. Again, from Boyle:

> "…warring against mankind, and against the more excellent part of mankind, the Christian church, the interest of their subtle Adversary must be extensively promoted,

by depreciating those compositions (the Manual), which, if reverenced as universally as they are received, would prove so destructive to his influence and designs."

Here Boyle points out that nibbling away at the Manual, whispering doubt of the Manual in the ears of the Christian church, is one of the Adversary's chief weapons in his war against God and mankind. He also points out that if the Manual was "reverenced," given the respect it is due, by as many as casually embrace it, the Adversary's power would be greatly diminished. In other words, the Manual is the Christian's battle plan against the Adversary. This plan, written by God, can only be weakened by man's interference. Any claiming Christian who willingly adopts this weakened plan plays right into the Adversary's hands.

Let me provide a few examples. I already touched on this one in "He Exists." Genesis 1: We don't argue "creation;" we allow the Adversary to draw us into defending "6 Days." Worse, we get caught defending their definition of 6 Days rather than God's. Let's look:

> Genesis 1:1 "In the beginning God created the heavens and the earth. 2. The earth (land) was empty and without form, and darkness was over the surface of the abyss, and the spirit of God hovered over the surface of the waters. 3. Then God said, 'Let there be light'; and there was light. 4. God saw that the light was good; and God separated (divided) the light from the darkness. 5. God called the light day, and the darkness He called night. And there was evening and there was morning, one day. **(end day one)** 6. Then God said, 'Let there be an expanse in the midst of the waters, and let it separate the waters from the waters.' 7. God made the expanse, and separated the waters which

were below the expanse from the waters which were above the expanse; and it was so. 8. God called the expanse sky (heaven). And there was evening and there was morning, a second day. **(end day two)** 9. Then God said, 'Let the waters below the heavens be collected (gathered) into one place, and let the dry land appear'; and it was so. 10. God called the dry land earth and the collection of waters He called seas; and God saw that it was good. 11. Then God said, 'Let the earth sprout grass: herbs bearing seed, and fruit trees on the earth bearing fruit after their kind with seed in them'; and it was so. 12. Out of the earth came grass, herbs bearing seeds of their species, and trees bearing fruit with seeds of their species, and God saw that it was good. 13. There was evening and there was morning, a third day. **(end day three)** 14. Then God said, 'Let there be lights in the expanse of the sky (heavens) to separate (divide) the day from the night, and let them be for signs and for hours (appointed times) and for days and for years; 15. and let them be light in the expanse of the sky (heavens) to shine light on the earth'; and it was so. 16. God made the two great lights, the greater light to have dominion over the day, and the lesser light dominion over the night; He also made the stars. 17. God placed them in the sky (heavens) to shine on the earth, 18. and to rule the day and the night, and to separate (divide) the light from the darkness; and God saw that it was good. 19. There was evening and there was morning, a fourth day. (end day four)"

We debate six, 24-hour days. We defend rotations around a sun that wasn't even created until the "4th day." As you can see, God decided when the "light" began and when it ended and "darkness" began. God called the lighted period "Day" and the period of darkness "Night." On the 4th day "God made the two great lights" and, as He would later create man in His image, He created "Day" in the image of the light of His Spiritual existence. He created the construct of time for man on the 4th day. Let's verify by taking a look at what the Manual says about when man's time has ended and God Re-Creates the world: "But I saw no temple in the city, because the Lord God Almighty and the Lamb are its temple. And the city has no need of sun or moon to shine on it, because the glory of God illuminates the city, and the Lamb is its lamp. By its light the nations will walk, and into it the kings of the earth will bring their glory. Its gates will never be shut at the end of the day, because there will be no night there." (Revelations 21:22-25) Clearly, God mandates time, not the other way around. But the world demands God explain a 144-hour creation and how He did it even though that's not what it says. Many Modern Christians are hiding in the back seat of that bandwagon. They're not? Have you checked your church's official position? Do they say God "created" man and woman and that He created man from the dust and woman from the man's rib? Do they say, "God…breathed the breath of life into his nostrils, and the man became a living being… (Genesis 2:7) (and from him) made a woman?" (Genesis 2:22) Do they say, "He spoke and it was so"? Or do they say something like, "God created man through the process of evolution?" Have they taken a "Theistic Evolutionary" position? Have they "Added to or Subtracted from" the Bible? Are they Heretics? Are they Nicolaitans? If you attend and support their doctrine, what are you? I will resist the urge to continue dismantling these positions.

However, I will offer you one piece of data published, not in Christian or "fanatical" literature, but the *Journal of Molecular Biology* and referenced in the book, *HERETIC – One Scientist's Journey from Darwin to Design* by Matti Leisola & Jonathon Witt:

> "Axe looked at proteins of modest length (150 residues)... He found that the ratio of functional proteins to nonfunctional gibberish was 1 in 10^{74}. He found that the odds of getting a protein with a particular function was 1 in 10^{77}. That's one protein capable of carrying out that function for every 100,000,000,000,000,000,000,000,000,000 ,000,000,000,000,000,000,000,000,000,000,000, 000,000 dead-on-arrival proteins." The book illustrates, "The number of atoms in all of planet Earth is estimated to be around 10^{50} – a huge number but one dwarfed by 10^{77}! The latter number is a billion times a billion times a billion times bigger."

For those who do not know, this process of developing "functional proteins" is the key to the success of the evolutionary process and must have been repeated not just once but over and over again. As the data show, this is a mathematical impossibility. (Who's the science denier again?) In an effort to defend their god, some would say, "That's where God comes in... Intelligent Design." But, let me ask you... why would God play such a looooonggggg game when He could simply do what He said He did and say, "Let There Be." While it is obvious God's design overflowed with intelligence, Proverbs says it was Wisdom that existed before time began and walked hand-in-hand with God through Creation. If you would like more of these facts, I do not resist the urge to dismantle in my post "The Omnipotence of Man." So, I ask again:

What is your church's position? What is yours? Even when the odds are this much against him, do you side with man and question God, demanding He explains Himself?

God created us. He has all Authority. He owes us no explanation. But let's look again. We could go all day reading through the Bible and pointing out miracles that we can't explain. Think about that… we can't explain. What arrogance or maybe delusion does it take to think that if God did explain Himself we could even begin to understand? No, the Bible is not The Autobiography of God. God gave us countless gifts, including Life, **Hope,** and Resurrection. Being a Compassionate, Loving God, He didn't leave us to figure it out all by ourselves; He gave us an Instruction Manual. "In the beginning God created the heavens and the earth." (Genesis 1:1) This is the very first thing God had Moses record. Obviously, God, angels, and the Spiritual World already existed. This Book was to document and instruct man from "the beginning" of the Physical World, from the beginning of our existence. What God tells us about Himself is only how it pertains to us. Christians allow the Adversary to demand an explanation of how God is God. Ridiculous! Christians accept the premise that the Bible is about God and should explain God's existence, God's thoughts, God's actions, God's power, etc. Again, Ridiculous! The Bible is and does no such thing.

The Bible isn't to tell us how and why God does what He does (other than His Love for us), but how and why we should do what we do. It tells us where we came from, where we are and where we are headed. It tells us what we've done wrong and what right is. It explains and demonstrates "Truth" from perspectives we can understand. It instructs us how to live in Truth and by Faith. Like any good manual, it tells us how to maintain a healthy existence and what happens if we don't.

As M'Clure stated, this Manual gives us the rules for our "probation" here in the Physical World. It guides us in preparation for entering the Spiritual World that existed before creation. It explains **Hope** and the choice we must make. Finally, with Manual in hand, He gives us time to make our choice. (2 Peter 3:8,9)

In case you're still not sure I have made my case, let's look at what John has to say as he closes his book on the life of Christ. Not referring to all God is, not to Creation, not to the lives of Abraham, Moses or Noah, not to Michael, Gabriel or God's Kingdom, just to the time of Christ's ministry. Not to the details of the Spiritual world behind all Christ did, just that which this Apostle experienced: "There are many more things that Jesus did. If all of them were written down, I suppose that not even the world itself would have space for the books that would be written." (John 21:25)

The other trick the Adversary has managed to pull off is that the Bible is written for the Believer and the Unbeliever alike. Another lie. Both common sense and the text itself say different. First, common sense. Up through Moses, the Scriptures had not yet been documented. God's people were to "witness" by word of mouth and lifestyle. When God gave Moses the tablets, the commandments contained were the "Law" given to His people. As you work your way through the Scriptures you will find that the "books" were written for God's followers to learn from and then demonstrate to the world. Solomon wrote an entire book about every experience he could find in the world. He documented his exploits and then reported back to God's people, "...there is nothing new under the sun" (Ecclesiastes 1:9) and "Everything is meaningless!" (Ecclesiastes 12:8) except God. He wrote this to teach believers not to wander from God's instruction (Ecclesiastes 12:13-14).

The New Testament is a compilation of letters written between believers to instruct them how to behave and how to deal with and witness to the world of unbelievers around them. In other words, how to be "In the World, but Not of the World." Boyle said: "I must observe, that the apostles, and other inspired reasoners in the Bible, are accustomed to use arguments, not to convince opposers, but to confirm believers… arguments it would be improper to urge against refractory (obstinate, stubborn) unbelievers." Paul didn't write to the city of Ephesus or the Temple of Diana, he wrote to "the church of Ephesus." He didn't write to the stranger on the road, he wrote to Timothy, a believer, on how to deal with false teachers and unbelievers. Common sense tells us **the Bible is an Instruction Manual given to God's people to teach them His ways and His Offer of Hope in Christ.** The Manual instructs us how to live a life In Truth, By Faith, and Through Grace.

Next, the text: "And even if our gospel is hidden, it is hidden only to those who are perishing. The god of this age has <u>blinded</u> the minds of <u>unbelievers</u> so they cannot see the light of the gospel of the glory of Christ, who is the image of God." (2 Corinthians 4:3,4) Christ told His apostles this, "The knowledge of the mysteries of the kingdom of God has been given to you, but to others I speak in parables, so that, 'though seeing, they may not see; though hearing, they may not understand.'" (Luke 8:10)

The unbeliever is not blinded to the Gospel because God does not want them saved. They are blind because they "must first believe that He exists." Let's just let Christ explain it:

> "A farmer went out to sow his seed. And as he was sowing, some seed fell along the path, where it was trampled, and the birds of the air devoured it.

Some fell on rocky ground, and when it came up, the seedlings withered because they had no moisture.

Other seed fell among thorns, which grew up with it and choked the seedlings.

Still other seed fell on good soil, where it sprang up and produced a crop—a hundredfold." Luke 8:5-8

Christ follows with, "He who has ears to hear, let him hear." I know we all understand this. We have all had many occasions in our lives where we talked to someone and, as the old saying goes, "talked until we were blue in the face" or out of oxygen. No matter how much we said or how much we explained what we said, the person to whom we were talking had already made up their mind, so, they could not hear us. Later, Christ translates the parable for us:

Now, this is the meaning of the parable:

"The seed is the word of God. The seeds along the path are those who hear, but the devil comes and takes away the word from their hearts, so that they may not believe and be saved.

The seeds on rocky ground are those who hear the word and receive it with joy, but they have no root. They believe for a season, but in the time of testing, they fall away.

The seeds that fell among the thorns are those who hear, but as they go on their way, they are choked by the worries, riches, and pleasures of this life, and their fruit does not mature.

But the seeds on good soil are those with a noble and good heart, who hear the word, cling to it, and by <u>persevering</u> produce a crop." Luke 8:11-15

In the book of John, Christ states it plainly: "Whoever belongs to God hears the words of God. The reason you do not hear is that you do not belong to God." (John 8:47) The reason they do not hear is that they do not Believe. Because they do not Believe, the instructions are not for them. Quick example. When was the last time you went into a store, say for a lawnmower, and said, "I really don't need the mower, but could I take the operator's manual home?" Now, you might say, "If I read the manual, I might decide to get the mower." True, but only if you acknowledged you had a lawn, that you needed to mow it, and that the mower could do what the manual says… that it is what it says it is. Once you believe and embrace ownership of the mower, the contents of the manual take on new meaning and particular relevance. Here's the rest of Hebrews 11:6: "…anyone who approaches Him must (first) believe that He exists and that He rewards those who diligently seek Him." We must "believe that He exists," <u>then we must</u> "diligently seek Him." It isn't that God doesn't want everyone to have what Scripture offers, to have Hope. In fact, the Manual tells us that God "…desires all men to be saved and to come to the knowledge of the truth." (1 Timothy 2:4) It's that our Creator knows how we work, that we won't hear unless we want the instruction and the discipline. And, as we have already said, it is only "Free Will" because He won't chase us down and make us take it. **We must choose to accept, first The Offer, then the instruction.** "I love those who love me, <u>and those who search for me find me</u>." (Proverbs 8:17) "For it is My Father's will that <u>everyone who looks</u> to the Son <u>and believes</u> in Him shall have eternal life…" (John 6:40)

Let's step back to where we started this section; "The Scriptures afford more light than the brightest human authors. In them the ignorant may learn all requisite knowledge, and the most knowing may learn to discern their ignorance." Paul, Boyle, David, and Henry agree.

From Boyle: "The apostle assures us, 'that whatsoever things were written,' even in the Old Testament, 'were written for our learning;' (Rom 15:4) and some places of Scripture so far abound with materials of instruction, that a striking contrast exists between them and human writings; the former containing more substance than words, the other more words than substance."

From Paul: "For everything that was written in the past was written for our instruction, so that through endurance and the encouragement of the Scriptures, we might have hope. Now may the God who gives endurance and encouragement grant you harmony with one another in Christ Jesus…" (Romans 15:4,5)

Previous to our quote, Boyle points out that the first words recorded in the Manual were "Let there be light." Boyle ties this statement to Psalm 104:2 (Lord)"You are clothed with splendor and majesty. He wraps Himself in light as with a garment" and in verse 24, "How many are your works O Lord!" In the 104th Psalm, David praises God's wisdom and providence in creation. He ends in verse 34 with, "May my meditation be pleasing to Him, for I rejoice in the LORD." Boyle points to David who confirms what Paul states plainly, "…everything that was written in the past was written for our instruction (meditation)." But Henry takes it one important step further:

From Henry: "The evening and the morning were the sixth day; so that in six days God made the world. We are not to think but that <u>God could</u>

have made the world in an instant. He said that, Let there be light, and there was light, could have said, "Let there be a world," and there would have been a world, in a moment, in the twinkling of an eye, as at the resurrection, 1 Co. 15:52. But he did it in six days, that he might show himself a free-agent, doing his own work both in his own way and in his own time,—that his wisdom, power, and goodness, might appear to us, and be meditated upon by us, the more distinctly,—and that he might set us an example of working six days and resting the seventh; it is therefore made the reason of the fourth commandment. So much would the sabbath conduce to the keeping up of religion in the world that God had an eye to it in the timing of his creation. And now, as God reviewed his work, let us review our meditations upon it, and we shall find them very lame and defective, and our praises low and flat; let us therefore stir up ourselves, and all that is within us, to worship him that made the heaven, earth, and sea, and the fountains of waters, according to the tenour of the everlasting gospel, which is preached to every nation, Rev. 14:6, 7. All his works, in all places of his dominion, do bless him; and, therefore, bless thou the Lord, O my soul!"

Henry makes an amazing point. Not only are the very first words written in Scripture there for our instruction as Paul and Boyle point out, but Creation itself was carried out in the way it was for that very same instruction. No wonder the Adversary's world would have us reject it! If a Christian truly believed in God, if we truly believed God is who He says He is, then wouldn't this be where we would stand? We wouldn't argue God Created in six days. We would declare, "God Created in six days because He chose to take six days to do what He could have done in a Word." David, Henry and I agree, we should Meditate on that Instruction.

CHAPTER 6

The New Religion &
The Fate of Empires

Merriam-Webster defines Integrity as: "firm adherence to a code of especially moral values: (or) Incorruptibility."

"Our conscience testifies that we have conducted ourselves…in the holiness and sincerity that are from God—not in worldly wisdom, but in the Grace of God." (2 Corinthians 1:12)

As we showed before, Sincere is defined as follows: "Pure, being in reality what it appears to be; not feigned; not simulated; not assumed or said for the sake of appearance; real; not hypocritical or pretended."

Why begin this section with these seemingly random quotes? Because the world has a new dominant religion and this religion has its own "Doctrines" and its own "Morality." I will take time to address this religion because it is Hope's greatest enemy. This religion has not only infected the world outside The Church but lives in most traditional and modern churches as well. It runs the scale from hiding as a sub-culture to being adopted into official written church doctrine and preached from the pulpit. We will look a little closer at that later. Here I want to explain this religion and its doctrine. I will expose this "Secular Morality" for what it is… and what it is not. I do this to warn you that if you accept and embrace God's Offer of Hope, this religion will not "tolerate" you.

I began this section the way I did because it seems only common sense that any "Morality" should contain Integrity and Sincerity. I mean, the word integrity is, by Webster's definition, "Adherence to a code of Morality." It also made sense to me that for Morality to be "Moral" it should be Real, it should be "what it appears to be," and, without question, it should never be hypocritical. I can't see you nodding, but I'm sure you would agree. After all, Paul says that a Christian's "Moral Values" are "Sincere" and "are from God," not the "world." Good thing too, because the Manual also says, "The world is passing away along with its desires, but whoever does the will of God remains forever." (1 John 2:17)

I want you to hear this because Secular Morality will not only tell you that the Rules required to receive The Offer of Hope are wrong but even hateful. This religion tells you that "tolerance" is love (even though, as I stated, if you Live Hope, they will not tolerate you). The Manual warns that to tolerate unsafe behavior does not Love as God defines it, but "puts a stumbling block" between them and Hope. Doubt I'm right? Secular Morality stands against God's Commandments. The Manual says this is how we "know" we have embraced The Offer... we have embraced Hope, "By this we can be sure that we have come to know Him: if we keep His commandments. If anyone says, 'I know Him,' but does not keep His commandments, he is a liar, and the truth is not in him. But if anyone keeps His word, the love of God has been truly perfected in him. By this we know that we are in Him: Whoever claims to abide in Him must walk as Jesus walked." (1 John 2:3-6) Remember, it was "Balaam, who taught Balak to put a stumbling block before the sons of Israel," (Revelations 2:14), and we know what happened to the Nicolaitans when they followed his example.

Before we take a look at the "love" this new Social/Secular Religion offers, maybe we should look at the Love God offers...

"God so loved the world He gave His one and only Son..." (John 3:16) The "world" – that's you and me! Who do you love that much? Who else loves you that much? Refresher: "He gave His only Son" equals "He Offers our only **Hope**." God so Loved? The Manual references God's Love nearly 300 times. Strong's says the words used are "agapē" and "agapaō." In reading both the definitions and the references I am quite confident in providing this definition for what Love Is: "Genuine affection for another by a deliberate act of will, in moral clarity, as a matter of principle." Secular Morality takes the parts of the definition and the references they like and "lets the rest go." Are you ready? Here we go!

We are all familiar with 1 Corinthians 13:4-8: "Love is patient, love is kind, etc… Love never fails." But what about 1 John 5:3: "For this is the love of God, that we keep His commandments. And His commandments are not burdensome."? Or Numbers 14:18: "The LORD is slow to anger, abounding in love and forgiving sin and rebellion. Yet He does not leave the guilty unpunished."? And who hasn't heard, "Love thy neighbor as thyself"? Even the world, and this New Religion, loves to throw that one around. But who can quote the context, the meaning? What about the 26 words that precede this quote: "For the commandments, 'Do not commit adultery,' 'Do not murder,' 'Do not steal,' 'Do not covet,' and any other commandments, are summed up in this one decree: Love thy neighbor as thyself." (Romans 13:9) Or the 57 words that follow: "Love does no wrong to its neighbor. Therefore, love is the fulfillment of the Law...Let us behave decently, as in the daytime, not in carousing and drunkenness, not in sexual immorality and debauchery, not in dissension and jealousy. Instead, clothe yourselves with the Lord Jesus Christ, and make no provision for the desires of the flesh." (Romans 13:10,13,14) That's right. Love is not an excuse to sin or to justify or "tolerate" sin. Love Is to "fulfill the law" with thyself and thy neighbor. This is the context of Romans 13. God "so Loved us" that "He gave His one and only Son" to Offer us **Hope**. Then, to help us "hear" and embrace The Offer, He gave us a Manual that says, "Avoid the fire," "Don't do these things," and "Don't put a stumbling block in front of your neighbor. Love them enough to warn them also."

As 2 Timothy 1:7 says: "For God has not given us a spirit of timidity, but of power, Love, and self-control." And 1 John 4:18 says: "There is no fear in Love, but perfect Love drives out fear..." **Love does not make us weak or tolerant of sin, just the opposite! Love gives us the power to stand up to sin and fight for our brother.** Love is born in the "Divine Truth" given to us by God; once we have "walked in that Truth," we can have "Genuine Love" for our brother. 1 Peter 1:22: "Since you have purified your souls by obedience to the truth, so that you have a genuine Love for your brothers, Love one another deeply, from a pure heart." How do we do this? John 13:34,35: "A new commandment I give you: Love one another. As I have Loved you, so also you must Love one another. By this all men will know that you are My disciples, if you Love one another." And John 15:9,10: "As the Father has Loved Me, so have I Loved you. Remain in My Love. If you keep My commandments, you will remain in My Love, just as I have kept My Father's commandments and remain in His Love."

Love for God **Is**: obedience to His commandments, "Faith in Truth." **Love** for our brother **Is**: having no fear, "obedience to the Truth" and expecting the same. **Love is**: showing "Genuine" affection for another by a deliberate act of will, in moral clarity, as a matter of principle.

I know, I know, I'm supposed to talk about Secular Morality. Don't you think as Christians, or even just honest people, we should take a good look at Truth before evaluating anything? From this Truth, we have a baseline from which to compare. First, let me say the popular use of "secular" is fairly new. It is the modern replacement for what used to be called "Worldly." In fact, what I call "Secular Morality" today, Tozer referred to as "Worldly Orthodoxy" when adopted by the church in his time. I don't know exactly why it changed; maybe it pointed too directly to the Manual and to Truth. So, now we can see that this "Secular" Morality of which I speak is actually "Worldly Morality" or based in the Physical World. Let's look at the Manual: "Do not love the world or anything in the world. If anyone loves the world, the love of the Father is not in him. For all that is in the world—the desires of the flesh, the desires of the eyes, and the pride of life—is not from the Father but from the world." (1 John 2:15,16) If we base our decisions and our behavior on the world's judgment rather than on God's, what will be our defense when Hope is lost? Paul says, "I will keep on doing what I am doing, in order to undercut those who want an opportunity to be regarded as our equals in the things of which they boast. For such men are false apostles, deceitful workers, masquerading as apostles of Christ. And no wonder, for Satan himself masquerades as an angel of light. It is not surprising, then, if his servants masquerade as servants of righteousness. Their end will correspond to their actions." (2 Corinthians 11:12-15) So, our purpose here is to look at this Social/Secular Religion and decide: are those who live this Secular Morality "deceitful"? Are they "masquerading as servants of righteousness"? Are they servants of the Adversary? We'll judge the "tree by its fruits."

What have these prophets of Secular Morality done for our children? After all, every "moral" society looks out for its children. Wouldn't you agree? Almost three generations ago they installed the idea that our children shouldn't talk to God in school. Apparently, it was against the freedom God gave the children He created. On that note, two generations ago they began to teach our children the "Theory of Evolution" as fact while at the same time declaring God's Creation as blasphemy to this New Social/Secular Religion.

In 1969, Secular Morality began a new movement that would sweep across the land like a storm. Today it is popular to name storms; the name of this one: "Easy, No-Fault Divorce." But this New Religion was protecting the children. What could be more moral than that? Let's smell the "fruit," shall we?

As a result of this storm, **divorce rates would soar to over 50%** and the expected negative statistics of "broken homes" right along with them: **31% of children from divorced homes were dropping out of school** and **33% of girls were getting pregnant.** The numbers for their counterparts in married households were 13 and 11%, respectively. These stats, referenced in the book, *Growing Up with a Single Parent: What Hurts, What Helps,* also showed **11% of males from divorced homes under the age of 32 ended up in prison** as opposed to only 5% from homes where the parents stayed together. But, hey, that's one book… *The Evolution of Divorce* (W. Bradford Wilcox, Fall 2009) refers to sociologist Paul Amato's (Pennsylvania State University) study of the issue:

> "The divorce revolution's collective consequences for children are striking. Taking into account both divorce and non-marital childbearing, sociologist Paul Amato estimates that if the United States enjoyed the same level of family stability today as it did in 1960, the nation would have 750,000 fewer children repeating grades, 1.2 million fewer school suspensions, approximately 500,000 fewer acts of teenage delinquency, about 600,000 fewer kids receiving therapy, and approximately 70,000 fewer suicide attempts every year. Amato's conclusion: turning

back the family-stability clock just a few decades could significantly improve the lives of many children."

Meaning: going back in time and Not implementing Secular Morality would improve the lives of many children. I don't know about you, but I think that fruit stinks! How bad does it stink? Even some whom I think might have trumpeted the move have had to admit:

> "Marriage provides benefits both to children and to society. Although it was once possible to believe that the nation's high rates of divorce, cohabitation, and nonmarital childbearing represented little more than lifestyle alternatives brought about by the freedom to pursue individual self-fulfillment, many analysts now believe that these individual choices can be damaging to the children who have no say in them and to the society that enables them."

This from a published work, *The Future of Children* (fall 2005), by a group of scholars at the Brookings Institution and Princeton University. These referenced stats are now more than ten years old. CDC studies show they have gotten dramatically worse. In 2018, *USA Today* mined the data from a recent CDC report, and this is what they found. The number of **self-inflicted deaths of white children between the ages of 10 and 17 increased by 70%** during the period studied (1999 – 2014). While suicides **among Black children** and teens are less common, their suicide rate showed **an even greater increase of 77%.** We have not had "fewer" of our children attempt to end their lives; instead, "successful" suicides have skyrocketed. Here are some more numbers from the CDC. **Girls ages 10 to 14 taking their own lives increased three-fold**; yes, a whopping 300%. **In 2013, the 2nd leading cause of death for 10 to 24-year-olds was suicide**. The number one cause was "unintentional" or accidental death, which includes everything from falling off a roof to a car accident. Note, 10 to 24 is the Gang age; fewer of these young people were murdered by someone else than chose to murder themselves. Almost 3% more of these 10 to 24-year-old young people ended their own lives than had them ended by all the major health diseases combined: Cancer, Heart Disease, Diabetes, etc. One more from the CDC: **in 2015, girls between the ages of 15-19 who committed suicide hit a 40-year high**. But it's worse than that. Secular Morality fails or refuses to see the obvious connection between these stats and another phenomenon that has developed since this "loving" move… school shootings. Is it that hard to see that the same thing that causes children to kill themselves sometimes plays out in violence against their peers? Do they take note that the vast majority of these kids killing kids choose as their last victim themselves? No. Instead, this new Social/Secular Religion will declare a little more "moral" judgment. They try to take away more "Endowed Freedoms" and further their agenda with the blood of our lambs. The result if they succeed will simply be the headlines changing from "school shootings" to school stabbings, bombings or, as we've seen, driver inflicted killings. The tool doesn't matter. These children will use whatever tool they can find to scream, "I am lost!" Finally, most who do look at the children themselves declare them "mentally ill." But they are not mentally ill, they are morally ill. A condition passed down to them from their parents, their "New Religion," their Secular Morality. "That's not fair!" Really? Why do they never talk about, much less connect, the term "Going Postal" and its origin to child attacks? The reference comes from adults first doing what the children now mimic.

For generations, we declared it morally wrong in the eyes of God to discriminate based on the physical characteristics of race or sex. Today,

Secular Morality has re-packaged that very same discrimination with the sheep's clothing of "diversity" and "inclusion." They teach our children that before they can be included, they must first be divided into groups. To make it even clearer for them, they equate physical differences, like race or sex, with mental differences, like "orientation" and "identity." We are raising our children in compliance with a world that consistently puts their idols before everything and everyone. They ignore when a society of experts like the **"American College of Pediatricians"** <u>says multi-genderism and trans-genderism supported in children is tantamount to child abuse</u> (*Gender Ideology Harms Children*, Sept 2017). They even up the ante and require our children to accept members of the opposite sex into their private spaces or face punishment. Then they tell them, "No means No" (which it does). They teach them it's right to kill unborn babies but wrong to call their peers a bad name! They tell them color doesn't matter and then ask them on every government form what color they are! They tell them your sex doesn't matter and then offer them special privileges if they are the right one! They tell them not to steal from their neighbor until they inevitably get their first paycheck and see that someone has taken some of their earnings and given them to their neighbor!

We send our children out into a world where the wolves of Social/ Secular Religion have not just blurred the lines of right and wrong but have erased them all together. The "Fruit" of this "Tree?" Our children have lost hope, and worse, God's Offer of **Hope** is unknown to them. Earlier we showed what God's Love Is: "Genuine" affection for another by a deliberate act of will, in moral clarity, as a matter of principle. Where are they supposed to get this "moral clarity" if not from us? How will they act out of "principle" if we don't show them God's Character? When will we teach them what "genuine affection" is? In a world ruled by "other gods," where our children are sacrificed on the altar of political correctness and Secular Morality, is it really that hard to figure out why they end their lives looking for any world better than the one they're in?

I could and was going to go on about all the ways this new Social/ Secular Religion takes away the inherent rights of "creators" (parents) that we talked about. How children can elect surgery, take a life, etc. and their parents don't even have the right to know. But when a parent supports their child if they want to take drugs to alter their "identity" or mutilate themselves with surgery, then those same rights become sacrosanct. I was all ready to roll on how the "loving" hand of this new Secular Morality has touched or maybe grabbed the throats of mankind in general, but if the fruit I've shown you about the children doesn't repulse you... what would?

What we have just read leaves no question that while this New Secular Morality claims to be looking out for our children, the opposite is true. This small sample reveals that Social/Secular Religion is Not "what it appears to be." Anyone who would declare love for another, all the time inflicting such harm, is not "Sincere" and is devoid of any "Integrity." In fact, as soon as studies and reports like those referenced come out, the deacons and disciples of this New Religion begin breakdancing. They spin, twist and distract with their fancy moves, speaking their "father's tongue" in an attempt to blind you to the Truth. Christ is very clear about children and the kind of people who would bring them such pain. Anyone who would turn a blind eye "...is passing away along with (the world and) its desires." (1 John 2:17) The world will be the world; the problem doesn't lie there. It lies on the other side of the Stained Glass that embraces their Secular Morality and discards God's Morality.

Where Does It Lead?

I want to point you to a study that shows that not only is Secular Morality a real thing but that it has risen through history as the final stage of "The life-expectation of a great nation." The study produced two published articles from which the author "...attempted briefly to sketch some of the kinds of lessons which I believe we could learn." I reference this attempt, so titled:

THE FATE OF EMPIRES

and

SEARCH FOR SURVIVAL

Sir John Bagot Glubb

In this writing, Sir John uses the word "Empire" to describe what we today refer to as a "Super-Power." Throughout history, power has been traded among these super-powers and traceable patterns have been formed. Sir John mined these data from each empire's historical record. Because Sir John was only familiar and fluent enough in 11 empires, these are the bases of his observations. He does state, however, that if others with adequate knowledge and understanding were to study the other great empires, this would result in a total of 24. It does seem reasonable to conclude that if the "standard pattern" was consistent among all eleven he studied, it would likely hold true to the rest.

From his study, Sir John did indeed find a standard pattern. His attempt was "...to trace—the periods of the pioneers, of commerce, of affluence, of intellectualism and of decadence." What he found was this: "The stages of the rise and fall of great nations seem to be:

The Age of Pioneers (outburst)

The Age of Conquests

The Age of Commerce

The Age of Affluence

The Age of Intellect

The Age of Decadence."

History showed that "Decadence is marked by:" (among other things)

"Frivolity

The Welfare State

A weakening of religion."

What did Sir John identify as the "High Noon" of an empire's switch from ascent to decline? – "Indeed the change might be summarized as being from service to selfishness." What did he find followed this period of "Affluence?" "Every period of decline is characterized by this expansion of intellectual activity." Yes, Sir John did define this "intellectual activity:"

"Perhaps the most dangerous by-product of the Age of Intellect is the unconscious growth of the idea that the human brain can solve the problems of the world. Even on the low level of practical affairs this is patently untrue."

What does the child of this marriage of "Affluence" and "Intellectualism" look like?

"In due course, selfishness permeated the community, the coherence of which was weakened until disintegration was threatened. Then, as we have seen, came the period of pessimism with the accompanying spirit of frivolity and sensual indulgence, byproducts of despair."

Sir John even gives us a little litmus test of such an age: "The heroes of declining nations are always the same—the athlete, the singer or the actor."

Brought on by this "Age of Intellect" is the final stage, "The Age of Decadence." Sir John defines: "Decadence is both mental and moral deterioration, produced by the slow decline of the community from which its members cannot escape." He continues: "Decadence is a moral and spiritual disease, resulting from too long a period of wealth and power, producing cynicism, decline of religion, pessimism and frivolity."

Until now these "death throes" of an empire produced something else:

"Some of the greatest saints in history lived in times of national decadence, raising the banner of duty and service against the flood of depravity and despair. In this manner, **at the height of vice and frivolity the seeds of religious revival are quietly sown.**"

Also stating:

> "It was inevitable at such times that men should look back yearningly to the days of 'religion,' when the spirit of self-sacrifice was still strong enough to make men ready to give and to serve, rather than to snatch."

Sir John concludes:

> "The life-expectation of a great nation, it appears, commences with a violent, and usually unforeseen, outburst of energy, and ends in a lowering of moral standards, cynicism, pessimism and frivolity."

Quickly, I want to address "The Welfare State" part of "The Age of Decadence," lest anyone be tempted to confuse "self-sacrifice" with this political term. I include the entire example included in this section to disarm any accusation of cherry-picking:

> "When the welfare state was first introduced in Britain, it was hailed as a new high-water mark in the history of human development.
>
> History, however, seems to suggest that the age of decline of a great nation is often a period which shows a tendency to philanthropy and to sympathy for other races (a distinction of individual, not individual value). This phase may not be contradictory to the feeling described in the previous paragraph, that the dominant race has the right to rule the world. For the citizens of the great nation enjoy the role of Lady Bountiful. As long as it retains its status of leadership, the imperial people are glad to be generous,

even if slightly condescending. The rights of citizenship are generously bestowed on every race, even those formerly subject, and the equality of mankind is proclaimed. The Roman Empire passed through this phase, when equal citizenship was thrown open to all peoples, such provincials even becoming senators and emperors.

The Arab Empire of Baghdad was equally, perhaps even more, generous. During the Age of Conquests, pure-bred Arabs had constituted a ruling class, but in the ninth century the empire was completely cosmopolitan.

State assistance to the young and the poor was equally generous. University students received government grants to cover their expenses while they were receiving higher education. The State likewise offered free medical treatment to the poor. The first free public hospital was opened in Baghdad in the reign of Harun al-Rashid (786-809), and under his son, Mamun, free public hospitals sprang up all over the Arab world from Spain to what is now Pakistan.

The impression that it will always be automatically rich causes the declining empire to spend lavishly on its own benevolence, until such time as the economy collapses, the universities are closed and the hospitals fall into ruin. It may perhaps be incorrect to picture the welfare state as the high-water mark of human attainment. It may merely prove to be one more regular milestone in the life story of an ageing and decrepit empire."

A couple of final notes about Sir John's study. First, the summary from which I quote is 26 pages long. The volume of the study itself or the two original publications I do not know. The quoted paper was published in 1976 as a plea to the world and a kind of warning to the two great "Super-Powers" of the time, The USA and the USSR. You may have noticed that the USSR no longer exists, bringing Sir John's documented fallen Empires to 12. Also, his study showed that the average "Life Expectancy" of an Empire is approximately 250 years. How old is the USA again? Finally, to those who would say that this is just the work of a "Christian Fanatic," let me say that I wouldn't confidently claim that Sir John was a Christian. He, in fact, points out that it is inaccurate to believe that "Idol Worship" was merely the worship of stick figures, but that the figures they worshiped were representative of something more. To them, this something more was a spiritual entity that held power and authority to set a moral standard to which they were obliged to live up to. It is to this religious moral standard that he refers when he states the "decline in religion." The empires that he studied were of different religions but had all at one time held a higher "moral standard" set by that religious belief. When the empires in their arrogance and self-centeredness began to create their own morality and discarded that of divine authority, they went from self-centeredness to self-destruction.

We have definitively shown that not only is "Worldliness" "Secular Morality," "Moral Deterioration" or whatever you prefer to call it; really, it is a "Spiritual Disease" that leads to the "Decline of Religion" and the inevitable "Fate of Empires" and "Fallen Man." But what happens when all the empires have had their time? When the only Empire left is Global? What happens when that Global Empire embraces this "man-made" Secular Morality and discards the one True Divine Authority?

"I revealed Myself to those who did not ask for Me;
I was found by those who did not seek Me.
I said, 'Here I am! Here I am!'
to a nation that did not call My name.
All day long I have held out My hands
to an obstinate people,
who walk in the wrong path,
who follow their own imaginations,
to a people who continually
provoke Me to My face…
They say, 'Keep to yourself;
do not come near me, for I am holier than you!'
Such people are smoke in My nostrils,
a fire that burns all day long.
Behold, it is written before Me:
I will not keep silent,
but I will repay;
I will pay it back into their laps
both for your iniquities
and those of your fathers…"
Isaiah 65:1-3, 5-7 (Also see Revelation 21)

CHAPTER 7

The Popularity Contest & You Shall Not Be Overcome

"Popularity has slain more prophets of God than persecution ever did." Vance Havner

"…though they knew God, they did not glorify Him as God or show gratitude. Instead, their thinking became foolish and wicked, and their senseless minds were darkened. Although they claimed to be wise, they became fools, and exchanged the glory of the incorruptible God for an image in the form of corruptible man…Therefore God gave them over in the sinful desires of their hearts…They exchanged the truth of God for a lie, and worshiped and served the creature rather than the Creator, who is forever worthy of praise! Amen." (Romans 1:21-25)

While writing this, I watched a docu-movie about a popular international "mega-church." I feel no need to separate them out because the sentiments have become all too commonplace in many of today's churches. The film held a common theme that was encapsulated in one sentence of one interview: "I come to this church because I don't feel judged." To that person and to everyone else I say if you enter a church or talk to a church member who claims Christ and you don't feel judged… LEAVE QUICKLY! As I worked to clarify my thoughts on this section, I drove by a church whose sign said, "an all-inclusive church," obviously meaning, "No judgment here." To those looking for a sheepfold and see a church with a sign expressing a similar sentiment… KEEP DRIVING!

This is another lie the world tells and too many churches accept: to be judged is negative. If we do not judge how far apart from God's character we ourselves or our "brothers" are, then how are we or they to correct the problem? By now you know I like to use imagery to make connections with Truth, so try this. Think of something you are good at, maybe something you might pursue as a career… Now, think of the person you believe has reached the "top" in that particular thing. For example, maybe you like to sing and you think you are quite good. You might believe Ariana Grande or Carrie Underwood are great examples of mastering that skill. If you were suddenly put in front of a crowd with one of them and asked to perform your skill, wouldn't you feel compared to the expert? Wouldn't you feel a little intimidated by their expertise? Might you think, "Seriously… I'm supposed to perform in front of all these people standing next to them?" Wouldn't you feel "judged?" In fact, wouldn't you be "judging" yourself in comparison to them? The only Truthful answer is yes. So why, in the presence of God, shouldn't we feel judged?

I not only feel judged when I walk into a "spirit-filled" church, I feel judged whenever I think about God's creation. Whenever I walk outside and enjoy the beauty of a tree or the blue sky. Whenever the spring breeze caresses my face or the sun wakes me in the morning, I feel the Love He has for me and I am painfully aware of how "short of the glory of God" I fall… I am judged (Romans 3:23). Whenever I consider Christ's choice as God to become and live as a man and to suffer at the hands of men. Whenever I contemplate the choice Christ made to sacrifice Himself for me, I know I am unworthy and I am judged. Whenever I feel the presence of the Holy Spirit and think about the great kindness of such a gift. Whenever my heart is broken by some physical world event and the Spirit lifts me up. Whenever I begin to feel lost and the Spirit shines His light on the path, I am ashamed of every doubt, every transgression, every thought against God's Authority, every sin… I am judged… and I am thankful. I am thankful for being made aware of any and all ways I tarnish the image of God in which I was created. I am thankful for the opportunity that judgment provides to remove that tarnish and regain some of that image.

"Let the peace of Christ rule in your hearts, for to this you were called as members of one body. And be thankful. Let the word of Christ richly dwell within you as you teach and admonish one another with all wisdom, and as you sing psalms, hymns, and spiritual songs with gratitude in your hearts to God. And whatever you do, in word or deed, do it all in the name of the Lord Jesus, giving thanks to God the Father through Him." Colossians 3:15-17

"I wrote you in my letter not to associate with sexually immoral people. I was not including the sexually immoral of this world, or the greedy and swindlers, or idolaters. In that case you would have to leave this world. But now I am writing you not to associate with anyone who claims to be a brother but is sexually immoral or greedy, an idolater or a verbal abuser, a drunkard or a swindler. With such a man do not even eat. What business of mine is it to judge those outside the church? Are you not to judge those inside? God will judge those outside. "Expel the wicked man from among you." 1 Corinthians 5:9-13

If someone claims to be your Christian brother or sister but they do not "admonish" you, the "word of Christ" does not "dwell" in them and they do not "Love" you as He does. If they tell you "words" don't matter, it's only your "deeds" that count, they are not acting "in the name of the Lord." If they don't "judge" you but tell you as long as you don't act on your "sexually immoral" thoughts, you are OK… "Expel the wicked man (or woman)" who takes on God's Authority. They are false teachers and the church that shelters them is not part of Christ's sheepfold.

Tozer addressed the flaw behind such teachings 60 years ago. In "What About the Ethics of Jesus?" from *The Set of the Sail* he wrote:

> "Back of such teachings lie several grave errors, <u>possibly the worst being the failure to distinguish the Church of Christ from the fallen world of mankind</u>. According to the Bible the human race is morally fallen, spiritually alienated from God, lost and under severe sentence of divine judgment. In sharp contrast to this, the Church is a body of regenerated persons who have withdrawn from the world in spirit and in heart and have thrown in their lot with Christ to own Him as Savior and to follow Him as Lord." "The teachings of Jesus belong to the Church, not to society. Society is sin and sin is hostility to God."

And in "We Need Sanctified Thinkers" from the same book:

> "A religious mentality characterized by timidity and lack of moral courage has given us today a flabby Christianity, intellectually impoverished… We spoon-feed this insipid pablum to our inquiring youth and, to make it palatable, spice it up with carnal amusements filched from the unbelieving world. It is easier to entertain than to instruct, it is easier to follow degenerate public taste than to think for oneself, so too many of our evangelical leaders let their minds atrophy while they keep their fingers nimble operating religious gimmicks to bring in the curious crowds." (part II) "Another generation or two of this and what is now Evangelicalism will be Liberalism." (part I)

While Tozer was well known for preaching on such issues, I remember him saying in one of his sermons that if the churches didn't recognize and acknowledge this mistake and reverse direction, that in the next couple of decades it would be too late. The churches did not listen; in fact, in the decades since those decades passed, they have doubled down.

Henry explains the relevance of the above Scriptures, which is easily applied to today's churches:

> "This was the general wickedness of the Gentile world, and became twisted in with their laws and government; in compliance with which even the wise men among them, who knew and owned a supreme God and were convinced of the nonsense and absurdity of their polytheism and idolatry, yet did as the rest of their neighbours did."

That really does sum it up! The world today has written its own morality and has "twisted it with their laws and government." Sadly, the churches, Manual in hand, know better but "(do) as the rest of their neighbors (do)." In an effort to be accepted by a world of which they were never meant to be a part, they "embrace the rules they like and let the rest go," leaving countless Lost Sheep lost. What's worse, like our example from the docu-movie, these sheep sit safely within the walls of modern churches never being judged, never being truly convicted and, therefore, never knowing what they need to confess or what repentance looks like. To you "false prophets, teachers and hirelings," you "wolves in sheep's clothing," God says:

> "If I say to the wicked man, 'You will surely die,' but you do not warn him or speak out to warn him from his wicked

way to save his life, that wicked man will die in his iniquity, and I will hold you responsible for his blood." Ezekiel 3:18

"...many of the leaders believed in Him; but because of the Pharisees they did not confess Him, for fear that they would be put out of the synagogue. For they loved praise from men more than praise from God." John 12:42,43

"He who is not with Me is against Me, and he who does not gather with Me scatters." Matthew 12:30

"You belong to your father, the devil, and you want to carry out his desires. He was a murderer from the beginning, refusing to uphold the Truth, because there is no Truth in him. When he lies, he speaks his native language, because he is a liar and the father of lies." John 8:44

I said earlier that I would return to the issue of False Teachers, Wolves and the churches over which they have authority. I also said that you should look at their written doctrines or documented beliefs and compare them to the Manual; if they vary from it, move on. This is a standard we have discussed as it applies to ourselves, so why is it one we would not apply to our church and its leaders? There are all kinds of defenses employed to stop us from doing so, "The pastor spent years in seminary" and "you just don't have the knowledge to understand the intricacies of theology" and many more that point to "learning" and man's accumulated wisdom.

"See to it that no one takes you captive through philosophy and empty deception, which are based on human tradition and the spiritual forces of the world rather than on Christ." Colossians 2:8

"...instruct certain men not to teach false doctrines or devote themselves to myths and endless genealogies, which promote speculation rather than the stewardship of God's work, which is by faith. The goal of our instruction is the love that comes from a pure heart, a clear conscience, and a sincere faith. Some have strayed from these ways and turned aside to empty talk. They want to be teachers of the law, but they do not understand what they are saying or that which they so confidently assert." 1 Timothy 1:3-7

"...you have known the Holy Scriptures, which are able to make you wise for salvation through faith in Christ Jesus. All Scripture is God-breathed and is useful for instruction, for conviction, for correction, and for training in righteousness, so that the man of God may be complete, fully equipped for every good work." 2 Timothy 3:15-17

"If you continue in My word, you are truly My disciples. Then you will know the truth, and the truth will set you free." John 8:31,32

2 Timothy 3 is one of my favorites because it really sums it up: "... the Holy Scriptures, which are able to make you wise for salvation through faith in Christ Jesus." There are endless numbers of books filling endless numbers of shelves to which you can dedicate your life reading and studying. You can dive deep into the thinking of religious philosophers and meditate on the sayings of the wise, but if your goal is "Faith in Christ Jesus" (walking in Truth), then the Manual "is useful

for instruction, for conviction, for correction, and for training in righteousness." Through the study and dedication to this book, "the man of God may be complete, fully equipped for every good work." Because "All Scripture is God-breathed."

Sadly, today many of the churches that are dressed up as secure and safe Folds are actually cleverly disguised Dens, as in Den of wolves. Contrary to the previously stated belief, these churches do judge, they just judge by the Secular Morality they have adopted instead of God's. This fact will be proven undeniable when you compare the **"Instructions, Warnings and The Rules"** gathered from the Manual with the samples of compiled Doctrines of various churches provided. You will see these churches play political word games that sound a lot like "it depends on what your definition of the word is, is." But, in the church's case, they will draw distinctions between believing and "acts" in that belief, even though the Manual says the sin, or offense to God, is in the mind preceding the outward act. I'm sure that even a new Christian would look to a church's stated doctrine on "Justice" and expect to find some reference to God's Justice as it is the foundation upon and the fabric of which all Christians and the churches they attend are to be built. I expect you will be as surprised as I was to find the bold stand taken in Social/Secular teachings and the complete void of the Manual on this subject. But this is the Truth about today's churches that will be addressed in a subsequent chapter. I only reference it here to show the sandy foundations of these false teachers. Once again, to you who seek a shepherd and to those who would claim that staff:

> "Do not be deceived: 'Bad company corrupts good character.' Sober up as you ought, and stop sinning; for some

of you are ignorant of God. I say this to your shame." 1 Corinthians 15:33,34

"…their thoughts either accusing or defending them. This will come to pass on that day when God will judge men's secrets through Christ Jesus, as proclaimed by my gospel… All who sin apart from the law will also perish apart from the law, and all who sin under the law will be judged by the law. For it is not the hearers of the law who are righteous before God, but it is the doers of the law who will be declared righteous." Romans 2:15,16 & 12,13

Once again, Tozer: **"We are not diplomats but prophets, and our message is not a compromise but an ultimatum."**

Once again, Havner: **"I'm tired of hootenanny religion, the new brand of Christianity that pagans do not feel embarrassed to join… I'm tired of hearing in our church bodies that we must get away from our humble beginnings, shake the hayseed out of our hair, and come of age."**

"Thou Shalt Not Be Overcome"

I think we are all led to believe, or we just assume, that to be a Christian, to live under the protection of God, means "the good life." Boyle discredited this thought when he pointed out that the success of Christianity itself was a miracle proof of God. He did so with the following facts:

Christ Himself suffered and was crucified and His apostles met the same fate. On the road to this end, they continued to tell the world about a Great Offer of a Great **Hope**. Saul lived a life of wealth, stature, pride, power, and comfort. When he became Paul on the road to Damascus that day, from a worldly view, the opposite became true. In fact, there may have been no one more ridiculed, tortured, jailed, and even killed than Paul. **Yet, "Gentile" unbelievers became Believers because they wanted what he had. Why is that?**

Acts 2:37 says that when Peter, a lowly fisherman, spoke, 3,000 "… were cut to the heart (means, "felt judged") and asked Peter and the other apostles, 'Brothers, what shall we do?'" In Acts 5 it says that the high priests and the Sadducees "…rose up with jealousy. They arrested the apostles and put them in the public jail." When the angels freed them and they continued teaching of Christ, the high priests wanted to execute them, but Gamaliel advised them, "Leave these men alone. Let them go! For <u>if their purpose or endeavor is of human origin, it will fail. But if it is from God, you will not be able to stop them. You may even find yourselves fighting against God.</u>" (Acts 5:38) Almost taking his advice, the apostles were beaten and released. Peter and "The apostles left the Sanhedrin, rejoicing that they had been counted worthy of suffering disgrace for the Name (Christ). Every day, in the temple courts and from house to house, they did not stop teaching and proclaiming the good news that Jesus is the Christ." (Acts 5:41,42) **Unbelieving Jews** looked upon and listened to these jailed and beaten men and **said, "What shall we do to get what you got?" Christianity spread. Why is that?**

Something else Havner said comes to mind, an illustration. The True Believer lives like this, "I've got nothing, I've got everything. What's the devil going to do with anybody like that? The devil says, 'I'll give you this and I'll give you that,' the Christian says, 'You can't I've got everything.' Then that makes the devil mad and he says, 'I'll take this away and I'll take that away,' and the Christian says, 'You can't I don't have anything!'" **This is what the unbelievers saw in the Apostles.** No matter what the devil put upon them, the world saw God in the men. In them, they saw a world beyond. A world that gave them "Peace, **Hope!** and Love." These men were a window into a Spiritual World the unbelievers had not felt "of (their) world." **The Apostles saw Christ Die, they saw Him Rise and they lived as if He were returning tonight!** Because of this, the Jewish and Gentile unbelievers wanted what Paul, Peter and the other Apostles had! Since the beginning, the world and even the "established" church have not only made it hard on followers of Christ, they often outright persecuted them.

God revealed to Lady Julian the Truth of this question:

> "'Thou shalt not be overcome,' was said full sharply, and full mightily, for sureness and comfort against all tribulations that may come. He said not, 'Thou shalt not be tempested (violently agitated); thou shalt not be travailed (labored); thou shalt not be distressed;' but He said, 'Thou shalt not be overcome.' God will that we take heed to His word, and that we be ever mightily in sureness, in weal and in woe (in good times and bad)."

I had a series of experiences recently that were, in Truth, inconsequential to this world or the Spiritual… other than the Truth they revealed to me that is. In these events, I made efforts to avoid and intercede in the suffering of another. In the end, these efforts averted some suffering but could not derail the ultimate end. As a result, I realized that in this world suffering happens and will continue to happen. Sometimes, even with our best efforts, we cannot avoid it. The physical world is the Adversary's and suffering is his M.O. What the Apostles and Christ

Himself showed us is that in this world the sheep are few and we live in a world that would see us harm. In the physical world's efforts to separate us from the Shepherd, not only will the Adversary's attacks continue, they will likely increase, and as the Manual says:

> "Do not assume that I have come to bring peace to the earth; I have not come to bring peace, but a sword. For I have come to turn 'A man against his father, a daughter against her mother, a daughter-in-law against her mother-in-law. A man's enemies will be the members of his own household.' Anyone who loves his father or mother more than Me is not worthy of Me; anyone who loves his son or daughter more than Me is not worthy of Me; and anyone who does not take up his cross and follow Me is not worthy of Me. Whoever finds his life will lose it, and whoever loses his life for My sake will find it." Matthew 10:34

In other words, some of the greatest attacks, the most hurtful "woes" will come from those closest to us who are "of" the world. In fact, they may, as they did for Christ and the Apostles, come from the very people who claim to stand for God – the churches. However, The Church, Christ's True Sheepfold will provide you Sanctuary, show you God's Love and stand with you in **Hope**.

Let me bring this where that mega-church and others of its kind do not: Free Will and Personal Responsibility. There are many reasons for what we experience in this world. One is simply the attacks of the Adversary. We have also mentioned MClure's reference to our probation. Yet another is purification and tempering, which is tied to our probation. This topic may be a book in and of itself, so let me just highlight the relevance.

Probation is a time given to those who violate the law to show that they regret their previous choices. They show this regret not by words but with actions. They actively stand against the temptation to violate them again. They actively resist the efforts of others to lure them back into violation. They actively live a life in compliance with the rules. The result of this testing and triumphing process is a purified character. In Christian terms, a return to the image of God in which we were created. However, while in this state, we will also be tested by the same forces and characters that formerly sought to divert us. Surviving or recovering from these attacks makes us strong for the next round. We are made stronger, our resolve is hardened, we are "tempered."

So, you can see the world "in" which we live will be full of "woes." We can also see that God will use those woes for a greater purpose if we let Him. But if God does not do evil, then where do these woes come from? If the Adversary has no real power, where does he get his ammunition? YOU!... OK, ME too. "When tempted, no one should say, 'God is tempting me.' For God cannot be tempted by evil, nor does He tempt anyone. But each one is tempted when by his own evil desires he is lured away and enticed. Then after desire has conceived, it gives birth to sin; and sin, when it is full-grown, gives birth to death." (James 1:13-15)

We love to point to the Adversary and say, "He made me do it." But that's not really true. He didn't make Adam or Eve do what they did... they chose to act against God. There are also times when we feel justified in blaming God for the evil in the world and its effects. But that wasn't and isn't His plan. His plan was to create paradise, create us in His image and then let us choose... and that's where the problem comes in. **We get to choose!** From those choices comes the world we live in.

Because there is only One who has always chosen perfectly, everyone else must feel the impact of the wrong choices in the world. Even the most devout follower of Christ falls and, from those falls, receives woe. Sometimes our falls and failures cause woe for others. Sometimes those others are followers of Christ. This being true, we must acknowledge our part in this world and take responsibility for our acts against God. For it is those acts and those acts alone that bring the woes we complain about and from which many Christians feel they should be exempt.

If we choose to ignore or act against the Instructions, Warnings and The Rules, then we should expect some woe in return. This is not God's choice; it is ours. Earlier we talked about how sin is not restricted to this list but is unique to each one of us. If we choose to do something that we believe is an act against God's Character, then we have sinned and should anticipate a response. Just to be clear, believing something on the list is not a sin does not make it not a sin. The list is established by God's Sovereign Authority; our personal beliefs can only add personal offenses to it. As Paul put it, "…everything that is not from faith is sin." (Romans 14:23)

If you will remember, I talked about the personal Peace, Joy and **Hope** I've had the last couple of years. I also talked about the onslaught that came with them. I didn't say that with revelation and spiritual growth came worldly blessing. True blessing comes at the time of our Reward when we cash in our Reservation. A life with God means a world in spite of the Physical, not without it. Until then:

> "Be strong in the Lord and in His mighty power. Put on the full armor of God, so that you can make your stand against the devil's schemes. For our struggle is not against flesh and blood, but against the rulers, against the

authorities, against the powers of this world's darkness, and against the spiritual forces of evil in the heavenly realms. Therefore take up the full armor of God, so that when the day of evil comes, you will be able to stand your ground, and having done everything, to stand. Stand firm then, with the belt of truth fastened around your waist, with the breastplate of righteousness arrayed, and with your feet fitted with the readiness of the gospel of peace. In addition to all this, take up the shield of faith, with which you can extinguish all the flaming arrows of the evil one. And take the helmet of salvation and the sword of the Spirit, which is the word of God." Ephesians 6:10-17

By the way… why would someone who is not expected to face battle need or be instructed to put on a suit of "armor?" Always remember, if you wear the described "Armor of God," **"Thou Shalt Not Be Overcome!"**

CHAPTER 8

Instructions, Warnings & The Rules

In 1 Timothy 1:5, Paul says to Timothy, "The goal of our instruction is love from a pure heart and a good conscience and a sincere faith."

"All Scripture is God-breathed and is useful for instruction, for conviction, for correction, and for training in righteousness, so that the man of God may be complete, fully equipped for every good work." 2 Timothy 3:16,17

"For the Gospel (Manual) reveals the righteousness of God that comes by faith from start to finish, just as it is written: 'The righteous will live by faith.'" Romans 1:17

"...this is my prayer: that your love may abound more and more in knowledge and profound insight, so that you can discern what is best, that you may be pure and blameless for the day of Christ..." Philippians 1:9,10

"...everything that was written in the past was written for our instruction, so that through endurance and the encouragement of the Scriptures, we might have Hope." Romans 15:4

We've discussed how the world around you has made great efforts to convince you that the Manual and any God who would hold us to its standard is hateful. I have just shown what God, through Paul, says about Himself and His Instruction Manual given to us.

Through John God says:

"Those I love, I rebuke and discipline. Therefore be earnest and repent." Revelations 3:19

...Like any good and loving parent would and should do.

And through Peter He says:

"Who will harm you if you are zealous for what is good? But even if you should suffer for what is right, you are blessed. Do not fear their intimidation; do not be shaken." 1 Peter 3:13,14

So, why is it so important that I Re-Set the vocabulary, that I provide you with God's clear warnings?

"Son of man, I have made you a watchman for the house of Israel. Whenever you hear a word from My mouth, give them a warning from Me. If I say to the wicked man, 'You will surely die,' but you do not warn him or speak out to warn him from his wicked way to save his life, that wicked man will die in his iniquity, and I will hold you responsible for his blood. But if you warn a wicked man and he does not turn from his wickedness and his wicked way, he will die in his iniquity, but you will have saved yourself." Ezekiel 3:17-19

But it's more than that. I couldn't put it any clearer or eloquently than Tozer in his sermon on the book of Jude:

> "…you cannot know truth about yourself unless you first know truth about God! You came from the hand of God and back to God you must go, for better or for worse, for judgment or for blessing… If I have a low conception of God, I have a low conception of myself and if I have a low conception of myself, I have a dangerous conception of sin! And if I have a dangerous conception of sin, I have a degraded conception of Christ! So, here's the way it works: God is reduced and man is degraded and sin is underestimated and Christ is disparaged!"

"Just then, a man came up to Jesus and inquired, 'Teacher, what good thing must I do to obtain eternal life?' 'Why do you ask Me about what is good?' Jesus replied, 'There is only One who is good. If you want to enter life, keep the commandments… Do not murder, do not commit adultery, do not steal, do not bear false witness, honor your father and mother, and love your neighbor as yourself.'" Matthew 19:16-19

As we just showed from Matthew, sometimes the instruction comes in the form of "do not's," sometimes as "dos" and other times as a list of things that are declared wrong, such as in Romans 1.

"Furthermore, since they did not see fit to acknowledge God, He gave them up to a depraved mind, to do what ought not to be done. They have become filled with every kind of wickedness, evil, greed, and depravity. They are full of envy, murder, strife, deceit, and malice. They are gossips, slanderers, God-haters, insolent, arrogant, and boastful. They invent new forms of evil; they disobey their parents. They are senseless, faithless, heartless, merciless.

Although they know God's righteous decree that those who do such things are worthy of death, they not only continue to do these things, but also approve of those who practice them." Romans 1:28-32

Because as Paul also says in Romans 1, "…what may be known about God is plain to them, because God has made it plain to them." (v19) In this section, I will continue pulling quotes from the Manual representing His Instruction, His Warnings, and His Rules. Because I agree with Tozer's principle that you should never take one verse and turn it into a doctrine, you will see some repetition as represented above where murder is listed in both. However, it is just as logical a principle that any instruction worth repeating should be seen as a warning or a rule. I will, for the most part, refrain from listing multiple times the same instructions given to separate churches except where such repetition might bring more clarity.

This chapter in no way should be viewed as a replacement for reading the Manual itself. In fact, you should see the connections between the verses and be inspired to study the verses and supportive information surrounding them. "I am anxious, that the fountain should not be neglected for the streams; and esteem it the mark neither of wisdom nor of gratitude, to prefer reading the word of God in any book, rather, than in His own." Boyle

To the "Saints in Rome" and You and Me:

(Positive Warning, "Avoid the Fire") "God 'will repay each one according to his deeds.' To those who by perseverance in doing good seek glory, honor, and immortality, He will give eternal life. But for those who are self-seeking and who reject the truth and follow wickedness, there will be wrath and anger." Romans 2:6-8

(Rule) "For it is not the hearers of the law who are righteous before God, but it is the doers of the law who will be declared righteous." Romans 2:13

(Instruction, Don'ts, and Dos) "…do not let sin control your mortal body so that you obey its desires. Do not present the parts of your body to sin as instruments of wickedness, but present yourselves to God as those who have been brought from death to life; and present the parts of your body to Him as instruments of righteousness." Romans 6:12,13

(Instruction) "Those who live according to the flesh set their minds on the things of the flesh; but those who live according to the Spirit set their minds on the things of the Spirit. (Rule) The mind of the flesh is death, but the mind of the Spirit is life and peace, (Warning) because the mind of the flesh is hostile to God: It does not submit to God's law, nor can it do so." Romans 8:5-7

(Instruction w/implied Warning) "...who are you, O man, to talk back to God? Shall what is formed say to Him who formed it, "Why have you made me like this?" Romans 9:20

(Instruction) "Do not be conformed to this world, but be transformed by the renewing of your mind. Then you will be able to discern what is the good, pleasing, and perfect will of God." Romans 12:2

(Rule) "We have different gifts according to the grace given us. (Instruction) If one's gift is prophecy, let him use it in proportion to his faith; if it is serving, let him serve; if it is teaching, let him teach; if it is encouraging, let him encourage; if it is giving, let him give generously; if it is leading, let him lead with diligence; if it is showing mercy, let him do it cheerfully." Romans 12:6-8

(Rule) "Love must be sincere. (Instruction) Detest what is evil; cling to what is good. Be devoted to one another in brotherly love. Outdo yourselves in honoring one another." Romans 12:9,10

(Instruction) "Be joyful in hope, patient in affliction, persistent in prayer. Share with the saints who are in need. Practice hospitality." Romans 12:12,13

(Instruction) "Bless those who persecute you. Bless and do not curse. Rejoice with those who rejoice; weep with those who weep. Live in harmony with one another. Do not be proud, but enjoy the company of the lowly. Do not be conceited. Do not repay anyone evil for evil. Try to do what is honorable in everyone's eyes. If possible, on your part, live at peace with everyone." Romans 12:14-18

(Rule) "...it is necessary to submit to authority, not only to avoid punishment, but also as a matter of conscience. This is also why you pay taxes. For the authorities are God's servants, who devote themselves to their work. (Instruction) Pay everyone what you owe him: taxes to whom taxes are due, revenue to whom revenue is due, respect to whom respect is due, honor to whom honor is due." Romans 13:5-7

(Instruction) "Be indebted to no one, except to one another in love, for he who loves his neighbor has fulfilled the law. The commandments "Do not commit adultery," "Do not murder," "Do not steal," "Do not covet," and any other commandments, are summed up in this one decree: "Love your neighbor as yourself." Love does no wrong to its neighbor. Therefore love is the fulfillment of the law." Romans 13:8-10

(Instruction) "...lay aside the deeds of darkness and put on the armor of light. Let us behave decently, as in the daytime, not in carousing and drunkenness, not in sexual immorality and debauchery, not in dissension and jealousy. Instead, clothe yourselves with the Lord Jesus Christ, and make no provision for the desires of the flesh." Romans 13:12-14

(Warning) "...watch out for those who create divisions and obstacles that are contrary to the teaching you have learned. (Instruction) Turn away from them." Romans 16:17

To the Church in Corinth and You and Me:

(Instruction) "...we speak, not in words taught us by human wisdom, but in words taught by the Spirit, expressing spiritual truths in spiritual words." 1 Corinthians 2:13

(Instruction) "The spiritual man judges all things…" 1 Corinthians 2:15

(Instruction w/implied Warning) "…since there is jealousy and dissension among you, are you not worldly? Are you not walking in the way of man?" 1 Corinthians 2:3

(Instruction) "Do you not know that you yourselves are God's temple, and that God's Spirit dwells in you? (Warning) If anyone destroys God's temple, God will destroy him; for God's temple is holy, and you are that temple." 1 Corinthians 3:16,17

(Instruction) "…learn from us not to go beyond what is written." 1 Corinthians 4:6

(Instruction) "I urge you to imitate me. That is why I have sent you Timothy, my beloved and faithful child in the Lord. He will remind you of my way of life in Christ Jesus, which is exactly what I teach everywhere in every church." 1 Corinthians 4:16,17

(Instruction) "I am writing you not to associate with anyone who claims to be a brother but is sexually immoral or greedy, an idolater or a verbal abuser, a drunkard or a swindler. With such a man do not even eat." 1 Corinthians 5:11

(Warning w/implied Instruction) "If any of you has a grievance against another (believer), how dare he go to law before the unrighteous instead of before the saints! Do you not know that the saints will judge the world? And if you are to judge the world, are you not competent to judge trivial cases?" 1 Corinthians 6:1,2

(Rule) "…do you not know that the unrighteous ones will not inherit the kingdom of God? (Warning) Do not be deceived: neither the sexually immoral, nor idolaters, nor adulterers, nor effeminate, nor homosexuals, nor thieves, nor coveters, nor drunkards, nor verbal abusers, nor swindlers, will inherit the kingdom of God." 1 Corinthians 6:9,10

(Warning) "Flee from sexual immorality. (Instruction) Every other sin a man can commit is outside his body, but he who sins sexually sins against his own body. Do you not know that your body is a temple of the Holy Spirit who is in you, whom you have received from God? (Rule) You are not your own; you were bought at a price. (Instruction) Therefore glorify God with your body." 1 Corinthians 6:18-20

(Instruction) "A wife must not separate from her husband. But if she does, she must remain unmarried or else be reconciled to her husband. And a husband must not divorce his wife." 1 Corinthians 7:10,11

(Instruction) "…whether you eat or drink or whatever you do, do it all to the glory of God." 1 Corinthians 10:31

(Instruction w/implied Warning) "…when we are judged by the Lord, we are being disciplined so that we will not be condemned with the world." 1 Corinthians 11:32

(Warning) "Do not be deceived: 'Bad company corrupts good character.' (Instruction) Sober up as you ought, and stop sinning; for some of you are ignorant of God. I say this to your shame." 1 Corinthians 15:33,34

(Instruction) "Therefore, my beloved brothers, be steadfast and immovable. Always excel in the work of the Lord, because you know that (Rule) your labor in the Lord is not in vain." 1 Corinthians 15:58

(Instruction) "Be on the alert. Stand firm in the faith. Be men of courage. Be strong. Do everything in love." 1 Corinthians 16:13,14

(Instruction) "…we fix our eyes not on what is seen, but on what is unseen. (Rule) For what is seen is temporary, but what is unseen is eternal." 2 Corinthians 4:18

(Instruction) "…from now on we regard no one according to the flesh. Although we once regarded Christ in this way, we do so no longer. (Rule)Therefore **if anyone is in Christ, he is a new creation.** The old has passed away. Behold, the new has come!" 2 Corinthians 5:16,17

(Instruction) "Do not be unequally yoked with unbelievers. For what partnership can righteousness have with wickedness? Or what fellowship does light have with darkness? What harmony is there between Christ and Belial? Or what does a believer have in common with an unbeliever? What agreement can exist between the temple of God and idols? For we are the temple of the living God." 2 Corinthians 6:14-16

(Instruction) "Therefore, beloved, since we have these promises, let us cleanse ourselves from everything that defiles body and spirit, perfecting holiness in the fear of God." 2 Corinthians 7:1

(Rules) "Whoever sows sparingly will also reap sparingly, and whoever sows generously will also reap generously. (Instruction) Each one should give what he has decided in his heart to give, not out of regret or compulsion. For God loves a cheerful giver. And God is able to make all grace abound to you, so that in all things, at all times, having all that you need, you will abound in every good work." 2 Corinthians 9:6-8

(Instruction) "For though we live in the flesh, we do not wage war according to the flesh. The weapons of our warfare are not the weapons of the world. Instead, they have divine power to demolish strongholds. We tear down arguments, and every presumption set up against the knowledge of God; and **we take captive every thought to make it obedient to Christ."** 2 Corinthians 10:3-5

(Warning) "I am afraid, however, that just as Eve was deceived by the serpent's cunning, your minds may be led astray from your simple and pure devotion to Christ. For if someone comes and proclaims a Jesus other than the One we proclaimed, or if you receive a different spirit than the One you received, or a different gospel than the one you accepted, you put up with it way too easily." 2 Corinthians 11:3,4

(Instruction) "Examine yourselves to see whether you are in the faith; test yourselves." 2 Corinthians 13:5

To the Church in Galatia and You and Me:

(Warning) "But even if we or an angel from heaven should preach a gospel contrary to the one we preached to you, let him be under a curse!" Galatians 1:8

(Warning) "Am I now seeking the approval of men, or of God? Or am I striving to please men? (Rule) If I were still trying to please men, I would not be a servant of Christ." Galatians 1:10

(Instruction w/implied Warning) "...you, brothers, were called to freedom; but do not use your freedom as an opportunity for the flesh." Galatians 5:13

(Instruction) "...walk by the Spirit, and you will not gratify the desires of the flesh. For the flesh craves what is contrary to the Spirit, and the Spirit what is contrary to the flesh." Galatians 5:16,17

(Instruction & Warning) "The acts of the flesh are obvious: sexual immorality, impurity, and debauchery; idolatry and sorcery; hatred, discord, jealousy, and rage; rivalries, divisions, factions, and envy; drunkenness, orgies, and the like. I warn you, as I did before, that those who practice such things will not inherit the kingdom of God." Galatians 5:19-21

(Instruction) "…the fruit of the Spirit is love, joy, peace, patience, kindness, goodness, faithfulness, gentleness, and self-control. Against such things there is no law." Galatians 5:22,23

(Instruction) "Those who belong to Christ Jesus have crucified the flesh with its passions and desires. Since we live by the Spirit, let us walk in step with the Spirit. Let us not become conceited, provoking and envying one another." Galatians 5:24-26

(Instruction) "…if someone is caught in a sin, you who live by the Spirit should restore that person gently. (Warning) But watch yourselves, or you also may be tempted." Galatians 6:1

(Warning & Instruction) "Do not be deceived: **God is not to be mocked.** Whatever a man sows, he will reap in return. The one who sows to please his flesh, from the flesh will reap destruction; but the one who sows to please the Spirit, from the Spirit will reap eternal life." Galatians 6:7,8

(Instruction) "Let us not grow weary in well-doing, for in due time we will reap a harvest, if we do not give up. Therefore, as we have opportunity, let us do good to everyone, and especially to the family of faith." Galatians 6:9,10

To the Saints at Ephesus and You and Me:

(Rule) "There is one body and one Spirit, just as you were called to one hope when you were called; one Lord, one faith, one baptism; one God and Father of all, who is over all and through all and in all." Ephesians 4:4,5

(Instruction) "…put off your former way of life, your old self, which is being corrupted by its deceitful desires; to **be renewed in the spirit of your minds; and to put on the new self, created to be like God** in true righteousness and holiness." Ephesians 4:22-24

(Instruction) "…each of you must <u>put off falsehood and speak truthfully</u> to his neighbor…" Ephesians 4:25

(Instruction) "He who has been stealing must steal no longer, but must work, doing good with his own hands, that he may have something to share with the one in need." Ephesians 4:28

(Instruction) "Let no unwholesome talk come out of your mouths, but only what is helpful for building up the one in need and bringing grace to those who listen." Ephesians 4:29

(Instruction w/implied Warning) "…do not grieve the Holy Spirit of God, in whom you were sealed for the day of redemption." Ephesians 4:30

(Instruction) "Get rid of all bitterness, rage and anger, outcry and slander, along with every form of malice. Be kind and tender-hearted to one another, forgiving each other just as in Christ God forgave you." Ephesians 4:31,32

(Instruction) **"Be imitators of God…"** Ephesians 5:1

(Instruction) "…among you, as is proper among the saints, there must not be even a hint of sexual immorality, or of any kind of impurity, or of greed." Ephesians 5:3

(Instruction) "Nor should there be obscenity, foolish talk, or crude joking, which are out of character, but rather thanksgiving." Ephesians 5:4

(Rule) **"For of this you can be sure:** No immoral, impure, or greedy person (that is, an idolater), has any inheritance in the kingdom of Christ and of God." Ephesians 5:5

(Warning) "Let no one deceive you with empty words, for because of such things God's wrath comes on the sons of disobedience." Ephesians 5:6

(Instruction) "…you were once darkness, but now you are light in the Lord. Walk as children of light, for the fruit of the light consists in all goodness, righteousness, and truth. Test and prove what pleases the Lord." Ephesians 5:8-10

(Instruction) "Have no fellowship with the fruitless deeds of darkness, but rather expose them." Ephesians 5:11

(Instruction) "…it is shameful even to mention what the disobedient do in secret. But everything exposed by the light becomes visible…" Ephesians 5:12,13

(Warning) **"Pay careful attention**, then, **to how you walk**, not as unwise but as wise, redeeming the time, because the days are evil." Ephesians 5:15,16

(Instruction) "Do not get drunk on wine, which leads to reckless indiscretion. Instead, be filled with the Spirit." Ephesians 5:18

(Instruction) "Speak to one another with psalms, hymns, and spiritual songs. Sing and make music in your hearts to the Lord, **always giving thanks to God the Father for everything** in the name of our Lord Jesus Christ." Ephesians 5:19,20

(Instruction) "…each one of you also must love his wife as he loves himself, and the wife must respect her husband." Ephesians 5:33

(Instruction) "Children, obey your parents in the Lord, for this is right. "Honor your father and mother, that it may go well with you and that you may have a long life on the earth." Ephesians 6:1-3

(Instruction) "…do not provoke your children to anger; instead, bring them up in the <u>discipline and instruction</u> of the Lord." Ephesians 6:4

(Instruction) "Workers, obey those with earthly authority over you, with respect and fear and sincerity of heart, just as you would show to Christ. And do this not only to please them while they are watching, but as servants of Christ, doing the will of God from your heart. Serve with good will, as to the Lord and not to men, because you know that the Lord will reward each one for whatever good he does…" Ephesians 6:5-8

(Instruction) "You in earthly authority, do the same for your workers. Give up your use of threats, because you know that He who has authority over them and you is in heaven, and there is no favoritism with Him." Ephesians 6:9

(Instruction) "…be strong in the Lord and in His mighty power. Put on the full armor of God, so that you can make your stand against the devil's schemes." Ephesians 6:10-11

(Warning & Instruction) "...**stay alert** with all perseverance in your prayers..." Ephesians 6:18

To the Saints, Overseers and Deacons in Philippi and You and Me:

(Instruction) "...dare more greatly to speak the word without fear." Philippians 1:14

(Instruction) "...conduct yourselves in a manner worthy of the gospel of Christ. Then,... I will know that you stand firm in one spirit, contending side by side for the faith of the gospel, without being frightened in any way by those who oppose you." Philippians 1:27,28

(Rule) "...it has been granted to you on behalf of Christ not only to believe in Him, but also to suffer for Him." Philippians 1:29

(Instruction) "Do nothing out of selfish ambition or empty pride, but in humility consider others more important than yourselves. Each of you should look not only to your own interests, but also to the interests of others." Philippians 2:3,4

(Instruction) "...**continue to work out your salvation** with fear and trembling. For it is God who works in you to will and to act on behalf of His good purpose." Philippians 2:12,13

(Instruction) "Do everything without complaining or arguing, so that you may be blameless and pure, children of God without fault in a crooked and perverse generation, in which you shine as lights in the world..." Philippians 2:14,15

(Warning) "Watch out for those dogs, those workers of evil, those mutilators of the flesh!" Philippians 3:2

(Instruction) "...know Christ and the power of His resurrection and the fellowship of His sufferings, being conformed to Him in His death, and so, somehow, to attain to the resurrection from the dead." Philippians 3:10,11

(Instruction) "...press on toward the goal to win the prize of God's heavenly calling in Christ Jesus. All of us who are mature should embrace this point of view." Philippians 3:14,15

(Rule & Instruction) "...**our citizenship is in heaven,** and we eagerly await a Savior from there, the Lord Jesus Christ, who, by the power that enables Him to subject all things to Himself, will transform our lowly bodies to be like His glorious body." Philippians 3:20,21

(Instruction) "**Be anxious for nothing,** but in everything, by prayer and petition, with thanksgiving, present your requests to God. And the peace of God, which surpasses all understanding, will guard your hearts and your minds in Christ Jesus." Philippians 4:6,7

(Instruction) "...whatever is true, whatever is honorable, whatever is right, whatever is pure, whatever is lovely, whatever is admirable—if anything is excellent or praiseworthy—think on these things. **Whatever you have learned or received or heard from me, or seen in me, put into practice.** And the God of peace will be with you." Philippians 4:8,9

(Instruction) "I have learned to be content regardless of my circumstances. I know how to live humbly, and I know how to abound. I am accustomed to any and every situation—to being filled and being hungry, to having plenty and having need. I can do all things **through Christ who gives me strength**." Philippians 4:11-13

(Instruction) **"God will supply all your needs according to His glorious riches in Christ Jesus."** Philippians 4:19

To the Saints and Faithful in Colossae and You and Me:

(Rule) "He has reconciled you by Christ's physical body through death to present you holy, unblemished, and blameless in His presence - **if indeed you continue in your faith,** established and firm, **not moved from the hope of the gospel** you heard..." Colossians 1:22,23

(Instruction) "...just as you have received Christ Jesus as Lord, continue to walk in Him, rooted and built up in Him, established in the faith as you were taught..." Colossians 2:6,7

(Warning) "See to it that no one takes you captive through philosophy and empty deception, which are based on human tradition and the spiritual forces of the world rather than on Christ." Colossians 2:8

(Instruction) "...let no one judge you by what you eat or drink, or with regard to a festival, a New Moon, or a Sabbath." Colossians 2:16

(Warning) "Do not let anyone who delights in false humility and the worship of angels disqualify you with speculation about what he has seen." Colossians 2:18

(Instruction) "...since you have been raised with Christ, strive for the things above, where Christ is seated at the right hand of God. Set your minds on things above, not on earthly things." Colossians 3:1,2

(Instruction & Warning) **"Put to death, therefore, the components of your earthly nature:** sexual immorality, impurity, lust, evil desires, and greed, which is idolatry. Because of these, the wrath of God is coming on the sons of disobedience." Colossians 3:5,6

(Instruction) "When you lived among them, you also used to walk in these ways. But now you must put aside all such things as these: anger, rage, malice, slander, and filthy language from your mouth." Colossians 3:7,8

(Instruction) "Do not lie to one another, since you have taken off the old self with its practices, and have <u>put on the new self, which is being renewed in knowledge in</u> the image of its Creator." Colossians 3:9,10

(Instruction) "...**as the elect of God, holy and beloved**, clothe yourselves with hearts of compassion, kindness, humility, gentleness, and patience." Colossians 3:12

(Instruction) "...forgive any complaint you may have against one another. Forgive as the Lord forgave you." Colossians 3:13

(Instruction) "Let the peace of Christ rule in your hearts..." Colossians 3:15

(Instruction) "Let the word of Christ richly dwell within you as you teach and admonish one another with all wisdom..." Colossians 3:16

(Instruction) "...whatever you do, <u>in word or deed</u>, do it all in the name of the Lord Jesus, giving thanks to God the Father through Him." Colossians 3:17

(Instruction) "Devote yourselves to prayer, being watchful and thankful..." Colossians 4:2

(Instruction w/implied Warning) "Act wisely toward outsiders, redeeming the time." Colossians 4:5

(Instruction) "Let your speech always be gracious, seasoned with salt (prudence), so that you may know how to answer everyone." Colossians 4:6

To the church of the Thessalonians and to You and Me:

(Instruction) "...our appeal does not arise from deceit or ulterior motives or trickery. Instead, we speak as those approved by God to be entrusted with the gospel, not in order to please men but God, who examines our hearts." 1 Thessalonians 1:3,4

(Instruction) "...live in a way that is pleasing to God... For you know the instructions we gave you by the authority of the Lord Jesus." 1 Thessalonians 4:1,2

(Rule & Warning) "For God has not called us to impurity, but to holiness. Anyone, then, who rejects this command does not reject man but God..." 1 Thessalonians 4:7,8

(Warning) "...you are fully aware that the Day of the Lord will come like a thief in the night. While people are saying, "Peace and security," destruction will come upon them suddenly, like labor pains on a pregnant woman, and they will not escape. But you, brothers, are not in the darkness so that this day should overtake you like a thief." 1 Thessalonians 5:2-4

(Instruction) "…acknowledge those who work diligently among you, who preside over you in the Lord and give you instruction. In love, hold them in highest regard because of their work." 1 Thessalonians 5:12,13

(Instruction) "…admonish the unruly, encourage the fainthearted, help the weak, and be patient with everyone." 1 Thessalonians 5:14

(Instruction) "Make sure that no one repays evil for evil. Always pursue what is good for one another and for all people." 1 Thessalonians 5:15

(Instruction) "Rejoice at all times." 1 Thessalonians 5:16

(Instruction) "Pray without ceasing." 1 Thessalonians 5 :17

(Instruction) "Give thanks in every circumstance, for this is God's will for you in Christ Jesus." 1 Thessalonians 5:18

(Instruction) "Do not extinguish the Spirit." 1 Thessalonians 5:19

(Instruction) "Do not treat prophecies with contempt, but test all things." 1 Thessalonians 5:20,21

(Instruction) "Hold fast to what is good. Abstain from every form of evil." 1 Thessalonians 5:21,22

(Warning & Rule) "…it is only right for God to repay with affliction those who afflict you, and to grant relief to you who are oppressed… when the Lord Jesus is revealed from heaven with His mighty angels in blazing fire." 2 Thessalonians 1:6-8

(Warning) "He will inflict vengeance on those who do not know God and do not obey the gospel of our Lord Jesus. They will suffer the penalty of eternal destruction, separated from the presence of the Lord and the glory of His might…" 2 Thessalonians 1:8,9

(Warning) "…judgment will come upon all who have disbelieved the truth and delighted in wickedness." 2 Thessalonians 2:12

(Instruction) "…stand firm and cling to the traditions we taught you, whether by speech or by letter." 2 Thessalonians 2:15

(Instruction) "…keep away from any brother who leads an undisciplined life…" 2 Thessalonians 3:6

(Instruction) "If anyone is unwilling to work, he shall not eat." 2 Thessalonians 3:10

(Instruction) **"Take note of anyone who does not obey the instructions** we have given in this letter. <u>Do not associate with him</u>, so that he may be ashamed. Yet <u>do not regard him as an enemy, but warn him as a brother.</u>" 2 Thessalonians 3:14,15

To Timothy... and You and Me:

(Instruction) "…instruct certain men not to teach false doctrines or devote themselves to myths and endless genealogies, which promote speculation rather than the stewardship of God's work, which is by faith." 1 Timothy 1:3,4

(Instruction w/implied Warning) "The goal of our instruction is the love that comes from a pure heart, a clear conscience, and a sincere faith. Some have strayed from these ways and turned aside to empty talk. They want to be teachers of the law, but they do not understand what they are saying or that which they so confidently assert." 1 Timothy 1:5-7

(Rule & Instruction) "…the law is good, if one uses it legitimately." 1 Timothy 1:8

(Rule) "…that law is not enacted for the righteous, but for the lawless and rebellious, for the ungodly and sinful, for the unholy and profane, for killers of father or mother, for murderers, for the sexually immoral, for homosexuals, for slave traders and liars and perjurers, and for anyone else who is averse to sound teaching that agrees with the glorious gospel of the blessed God…" 1 Timothy 1:9-11

(Rule & Instruction) "**This is a trustworthy saying, worthy of full acceptance**: Christ Jesus came into the world to save sinners, of whom I am the worst. But for this very reason I was shown mercy, so that in me, the worst of sinners, Christ Jesus might display His perfect patience as an example to those who would believe in Him for eternal life." 1 Timothy 1:15,16

(Instruction) "I urge that petitions, prayers, intercessions, and thanksgiving be offered on behalf of all men…" 1 Timothy 2:1

(Instruction) "**God our Savior,… desires all men to be saved** and to come to the knowledge of the truth." 1 Timothy 2:3,4

(Rule) "…there is one God and one mediator between God and men, the man Christ Jesus, who gave Himself as a ransom for all…" 1 Timothy 2:5,6

(Instruction) "I want the men everywhere to pray, lifting up holy hands, without anger or dissension." 1 Timothy 2:8

(Instruction) "Likewise, I want the women to adorn themselves with respectable apparel, with modesty, and with self-control,…with good deeds, as is proper for women who profess to worship God." 1 Timothy 2:9,10

(Warning) "If anyone teaches another doctrine and disagrees with the sound words of our Lord Jesus Christ he is conceited and understands nothing. Instead, he has an unhealthy interest in controversies and semantics, out of which come envy, strife, abusive talk, evil suspicions, and constant friction between men of depraved mind who are devoid of the truth." 1 Timothy 6:3-5

(Instruction) "…godliness with contentment is great gain." 1 Timothy 6:6

(Rule) "For we brought nothing into the world, and neither can we carry anything out." 1 Timothy 6:7

(Instruction) "…the love of money is the root of all kinds of evil. (Warning) By craving it, some have wandered away from the faith and pierced themselves with many sorrows." 1 Timothy 6:10

(Instruction) "O man of God, flee from these things and pursue righteousness, godliness, faith, love, perseverance, and gentleness." 1 Timothy 6:11

(Instruction) **"Fight the good fight of the faith.** Take hold of the eternal life to which you were called when you made the good confession…" 1 Timothy 6:12

(Instruction) "Instruct those who are rich in the present age not to be conceited and not to put their hope in the uncertainty of wealth, but in God, who richly provides all things for us to enjoy." 1 Timothy 6:17

(Instruction) "Instruct them to do good, to be rich in good works, and to be generous and ready to share, treasuring up for themselves a firm foundation for the future, so that they may take hold of that which is truly life." 1 Timothy 6:18,19

(Instruction) "…do not be ashamed of the testimony of our Lord…" 2 Timothy 1:8

(Instruction) "Make every effort to present yourself approved to God, an unashamed workman who accurately handles the word of truth." 2 Timothy 2:15

(Rule) **"God's firm foundation stands, bearing this seal:** "The Lord knows those who are His," and, "Everyone who calls on the name of the Lord must turn away from iniquity." 2 Timothy 2:19

(Rule) "…a servant of the Lord must not be quarrelsome, but must be kind to everyone, able to teach, and patient." 2 Timothy 2:24

(Rule) "…(a servant of the Lord) must humbly instruct those who oppose him, in the hope that God may grant them repentance leading to a knowledge of the truth; that they may come to their senses and escape the Devil's trap, having been captured by him to do his will." 2 Timothy 2:25

(Warning) "…**understand this:** In the last days terrible times will come. For men will be lovers of themselves, lovers of money, boastful, arrogant, abusive, disobedient to their parents, ungrateful, unholy, unloving, unforgiving, slanderous, without self-control, brutal, without love of good, traitorous, reckless, conceited, lovers of pleasure rather than lovers of God, having a form of godliness but denying its power. Turn away from such as these!" 2 Timothy 3:1-5

(Warning) "…all who desire to live godly lives in Christ Jesus will be persecuted, while evil men and imposters go from bad to worse, deceiving and being deceived." 2 Timothy 3:12,13

(Instruction) "<u>All</u> Scripture is God-breathed and is useful for instruction, for conviction, for correction, and for training in righteousness, so that the man of God may be complete, fully equipped for every good work." 2 Timothy 3:16,17

To Titus and You and Me:

(Rule & Warning) "To the pure, all things are pure; but to the defiled and unbelieving, nothing is pure. Indeed, both their minds and their consciences are defiled. They profess to know God, but they deny Him by their actions. They are detestable, disobedient, and unfit for any good deed." Titus 1:15,16

(Instruction) "In everything, show yourself to be an example by doing good works. In your teaching show integrity, dignity, and wholesome speech that is above reproach, so that anyone who opposes us will be ashamed that he has nothing bad to say about us." Titus 2:7,8

(Instruction) "**…the Grace of God** has appeared, bringing salvation to all men. It **instructs us to renounce ungodliness and worldly passions,** and to live sensible, upright, and godly lives in the present age, **as we await the blessed hope** and glorious appearance of our great God and Savior, Jesus Christ." Titus 2:11-13

(Instruction) "Remind the believers to be subject to rulers and authorities, to be obedient and ready for every good work, to malign no one, and to be peaceable and gentle, showing full consideration to everyone." Titus 3:1,2

(Instruction) "…avoid foolish controversies, genealogies, arguments, and quarrels about the law, because these things are pointless and worthless." Titus 3:9

(Instruction w/implied Warning) "Reject a divisive man after a first and second admonition, knowing that such a man is corrupt and sinful; he is self-condemned." Titus 3:10,11

To the Hebrews and You and Me:

(Rule) "God subjected all things to him, He left nothing outside of his control. Yet at present we do not see everything subject to him." Hebrews 2:8

(Instruction) "See to it, brothers, that none of you has a wicked heart of unbelief that turns away from the living God." Hebrews 3:12

(Instruction) "…exhort one another daily, as long as it is called today, so that none of you may be hardened by sin's deceitfulness." Hebrews 3:13

(Rule) "…the word of God is living and active…It judges the thoughts and intentions of the heart." Hebrews 4:12

(Warning, Instruction & Rule) "…show this same diligence to the very end, in order to make your **hope** sure. Then you will not be sluggish, but will imitate those who through faith and patience inherit what has been promised." Hebrews 6:11,12

(Rule) "**…it is impossible for God to lie**, (Instruction) we who have fled to take hold of the **hope** set before us may be strongly encouraged." Hebrews 6:18

(Instruction) "…hold resolutely to the **hope** we profess, (Rule) for He who promised is faithful." Hebrews 10:23

(Instruction) "…consider how to spur one another on to love and good deeds." Hebrews 10:24

(Instruction) "Let us not neglect meeting together, as some have made a habit, but let us encourage one another, and all the more as you see the Day approaching." Hebrews 10:25

(Warning) **"If we deliberately go on sinning** after we have received the knowledge of the truth, no further sacrifice for sins remains, but only a fearful expectation of judgment and of raging fire that will consume all adversaries." Hebrews 10:26,27

(Warning) "Anyone who rejected the law of Moses died without mercy on the testimony of two or three witnesses. **How much more severely do you think one deserves to be punished who has trampled on the Son of God**, profaned the blood of the covenant that sanctified him, and insulted the Spirit of grace?" Hebrews 10:28,29

(Instruction) "…do not throw away your confidence; it holds a great reward. **You need to persevere**, so that after you have done the will of God, you will receive what He has promised." Hebrews 10:35,36

(Warning) **"My righteous one will live by faith**; and if he shrinks back, I will take no pleasure in him." Hebrews 10:38

(Rule) "…without faith it is impossible to please God, because anyone who approaches Him must believe that He exists and that He rewards those who earnestly seek Him." Hebrews 11:6

(Instruction) "…throw off every encumbrance and the sin that so easily entangles, and let us run with endurance the race set out for us." Hebrews 12:1

(Instruction) "…fix our eyes on Jesus, the author and perfecter of our faith…" Hebrews 12:2

(Warning) "**…do not take lightly the discipline of the Lord**, (Instruction) and do not lose heart when He rebukes you. (Rule) **For the Lord disciplines the one He loves**, and He chastises every son He receives." Hebrews 12:5,6

(Instruction) "**Endure suffering as discipline**; God is treating you as sons. For what son is not disciplined by his father?...we have all had earthly fathers who disciplined us, and we respected them. Should we not much more submit to the Father of our spirits and live?" Hebrews 12:7,9

(Instruction) "God disciplines us for our good, so that we may share in His holiness." Hebrews 12:10

(Instruction) "…since we are receiving an unshakable kingdom, let us be filled with gratitude, and so worship God acceptably with reverence and awe." Hebrews 12:28

(Instruction) "Do not neglect to show hospitality to strangers…" Hebrews 13:2

(Warning) "Marriage should be honored by all and the marriage bed kept undefiled, for God will judge the sexually immoral and adulterers." Hebrews 13:4

(Instruction & Rule) "The Lord is my helper; I will not be afraid. What can man do to me?" Hebrews 13:6

(Instruction) "Remember your leaders <u>who spoke the word of God</u> to you. Consider the outcome of their way of life and imitate their faith. (Rule) **Jesus Christ is the same yesterday and today and forever.**" Hebrews 13:7,8

(Warning) "Do not be carried away by all kinds of strange teachings…" Hebrews 13:9

(Rule) "…here we do not have a permanent city, but we are looking for the city that is to come." Hebrews 13:14

(Instruction) "…**continually offer to God a sacrifice of praise**, the fruit of lips that confess His name." Hebrews 13:15

To the Twelve Tribes and You and Me:

(Instruction) "…if any of you lacks wisdom, he should **ask God, who gives generously** to all without finding fault, and it will be given to him. (Rule) <u>But he must ask in faith, without doubting</u>, because he who doubts is like a wave of the sea, blown and tossed by the wind. (Warning) That man should not expect to receive anything from the Lord. He is a double-minded man, unstable in all his ways." James 1:5-8

(Instruction) "When tempted, no one should say, 'God is tempting me.' (Rule) For God cannot be tempted by evil, nor does He tempt anyone." James 1:13

(Instruction) "Everyone should be quick to listen, slow to speak, and slow to anger…" James 1:19

(Instruction) "…get rid of all moral filth and every expression of evil, and humbly receive the word planted in you, which can save your souls." James 1:21

(Instruction) "Be doers of the word, and not hearers only. Otherwise, you are deceiving yourselves." James 1:22

(Warning) "If anyone considers himself religious and yet does not bridle his tongue, he deceives his heart and his religion is worthless." James 1:26

(Instruction) "Pure and undefiled religion before our God and Father is this: to care for orphans and widows in their distress, and to keep oneself from being polluted by the world." James 1:27

(Rule) "Whoever keeps the whole law but stumbles at just one point is guilty of breaking all of it." James 2:10

(Rule) "…faith by itself, if it is not complemented by action, is dead." James 2:17

(Rule) "…whoever chooses to be a friend of the world renders himself an enemy of God." James 4:4

(Rule) "God opposes the proud and arrogant (haughty), but gives grace to the humble." James 4:6

(Instruction) "**Submit** yourselves, then, **to God**. Resist the devil, and he will flee from you." James 4:7

(Instruction) "**Draw near to God**, and He will draw near to you." James 4:8

(Instruction) "Cleanse your hands, you sinners, and **purify your hearts**, you double-minded." James 4:8

(Instruction) "**Humble yourselves before the Lord**, and He will exalt you." James 4:10

(Rule) "**...whoever knows the right thing to do, yet fails to do it, is guilty of sin.**" James 4:17

(Instruction) "...do not swear, not by heaven or earth or by any other oath. Simply let your 'Yes' be yes, and your 'No,' no..." James 5:12

(Rule) "...the prayer offered in faith will restore the one who is sick. The Lord will raise him up. If he has sinned, he will be forgiven." James 5:15

(Instruction) "...confess your sins to each other and pray for each other so that you may be healed." James 5:16

(Rule w/implied Instruction) "**Whoever turns a sinner from the error of his way will save his soul from death...**" James 5:20

To the exiles in Pontus, Galatia, Cappadocia, Asia, Bithynia and you and me:

(Instruction) "...prepare your minds for action. Be sober-minded." 1 Peter 1:13

(Instruction) "Set your **hope** fully on the grace to be given you at the revelation of Jesus Christ." 1 Peter 1:13

(Instruction) "As obedient children, do not conform to the passions of your former ignorance." 1 Peter 1:14

(Instruction) "...just as He who called you is holy, so be holy in all you do..." 1 Peter 1:15

(Instruction) "Like newborn babies, crave pure spiritual milk, so that by it you may grow up in your salvation, now that you have tasted that the Lord is good." 1 Peter 2:2,3

(Instruction) "**Live in freedom**, (Warning) but do not use your freedom as a cover-up for evil; live as servants of God." 1 Peter 2:16

(Instruction) "Treat everyone with high regard: Love the brotherhood of believers, fear God, honor the king." 1 Peter 2:17

(Rule) "If you are insulted for the name of Christ, you are blessed, because the Spirit of glory and of God rests on you. (Instruction) Indeed, none of you should suffer as a murderer or thief or wrongdoer, or even as a meddler. But **if you suffer as a Christian**, do not be ashamed, but glorify God that you bear that name." 1 Peter 4:14-16

(Instruction) "...those who suffer according to God's will should entrust their souls to their faithful Creator and continue to do good." 1 Peter 4:19

(Instruction) "...clothe yourselves with humility toward one another..." 1 Peter 5:5

(Rule) "...God opposes the proud, but gives grace to the humble." 1 Peter 5:5

(Instruction) "Humble yourselves, therefore, under God's mighty hand, so that in due time He may exalt you." 1 Peter 5:6

(Instruction) **"Cast all your anxiety on Him, because He cares for you."** 1 Peter 5:7

(Warning) "Be sober-minded and alert. Your adversary the devil prowls around like a roaring lion, seeking someone to devour." 1 Peter 5:8

(Instruction) "…**make every effort** to add to your faith virtue; and to virtue, knowledge; and to knowledge, self-control; and to self-control, perseverance; and to perseverance, godliness; and to godliness, brotherly kindness; and to brotherly kindness, love. For if you possess these qualities and continue to grow in them, they will keep you from being ineffective and unproductive in your knowledge of our Lord Jesus Christ…if you practice these things you will never stumble, and you will receive a lavish reception into the eternal kingdom of our Lord and Savior Jesus Christ." 2 Peter 1:5-8-11

(Instruction) "…we did not follow cleverly devised fables when we made known to you the power and coming of our Lord Jesus Christ, but **we were eyewitnesses of His majesty**." 2 Peter 1:16

(Instruction) "We also have the word of the prophets (old testament) as confirmed beyond doubt. And you will do well to pay attention to it, as to a lamp shining in a dark place, until the day dawns and the morning star rises in your hearts." 1 Peter 1:19

(Rule) "…you must understand that no prophecy of Scripture comes from one's own interpretation. For no prophecy was ever brought forth by the will of man, but men spoke from God as they were carried along by the Holy Spirit." 1 Peter 1:20,21

"...if God did not spare the angels when they sinned, but cast them deep into hell, placing them in chains of darkness to be held for judgment; if He did not spare the ancient world...if He condemned the cities of Sodom and Gomorrah to destruction...if He rescued Lot, a righteous man distressed by the depraved conduct of the lawless...if all this is so, then <u>the Lord knows how to rescue the godly from trials and to hold the unrighteous for punishment on the day of judgment</u>." 2 Peter 2:4-9

(Rule w/implied Warning) "...a man is a slave to whatever has mastered him." 2 Peter 2:19

(Instruction) "**...do not let this one thing escape your notice:** (Rule) With the Lord a day is like a thousand years, and a thousand years are like a day. The Lord is not slow to fulfill His promise as some understand slowness, but is patient with you, not wanting anyone to perish but everyone to come to repentance." 2 Peter 3:8,9

(Warning) "...the Day of the Lord will come like a thief. The heavens will disappear with a roar, the elements will be destroyed by fire, and the earth and its works will be laid bare." 2 Peter 3:10

(Instruction) "Since everything will be destroyed in this way, what kind of people ought you to be? You ought to conduct yourselves in holiness and godliness...But in keeping with God's promise, we are looking forward to a new heaven and a new earth, where righteousness dwells." 2 Peter 3:11,13

(Instruction) "...as you anticipate these things, make every effort to be found at peace with Him, without spot or blemish." 2 Peter 3:14

(Warning) "Therefore, beloved, since you already know these things, **be on your guard** so that you will not be carried away by the error of the lawless and fall from your secure standing." 2 Peter 3:17

To "The Church" including You and Me:

(Instruction) "**...this is the message** we have heard from Him and announce to you: God is light, and in Him there is no darkness at all. If we say we have fellowship with Him yet walk in the darkness, we lie and do not practice the truth." 1 John 1:5,6

(Instruction) "If we say we have no sin, we deceive ourselves, and the truth is not in us." 1 John 1:8

(Instruction) "If we confess our sins, He is faithful and just to forgive us our sins and to cleanse us from all unrighteousness." 1 John 1:9

(Rule) "Whoever claims to abide in Him must walk as Jesus walked." 1 John2:6

(Instruction) "Do not love the world or anything in the world. (Rule) If anyone loves the world, the love of the Father is not in him." 1 John 2:15

(Rule) "Whoever denies the Son does not have the Father, but whoever confesses the Son has the Father also." 1 John 2:23

(Warning) "...do not believe every spirit, but test the spirits to see whether they are from God. For many false prophets have gone out into the world." 1 John 4:1

(Instruction) "...this is the love of God, that we keep His commandments. And His commandments are not burdensome, because everyone born of God overcomes the world. And this is the victory that has overcome the world: our faith." 1 John 5:3,4

(Instruction) "…this is the confidence that we have before Him: <u>If we ask anything according to His will</u>, He hears us. And if we know that He hears us in whatever we ask, we know that we already possess what we have asked of Him." 1 John 5:14,15

(Instruction) "…do not imitate what is evil, but what is good. The one who does good is of God; the one who does evil has not seen God." 3 John 1:11

(Instruction) "…have mercy on those who doubt; save others by snatching them from the fire; and to still others, show mercy tempered with fear, hating even the clothing stained by the flesh." Jude 1:22,23

To the Seven Churches and You and Me:

(Rule) "**He who has an ear**, let him hear what the Spirit says to the churches. To the one who is victorious, I will grant the right to eat from the tree of life in the Paradise of God." Revelations 2:7

(Instruction) "Be faithful even unto death, and I will give you the crown of life." Revelations 2:10

(Rule) "**He who has an ear**, let him hear what the Spirit says to the churches. The one who is victorious will not be harmed by the second death." Revelations 2:11

(Rule) "**He who has an ear**, let him hear what the Spirit says to the churches. To the one who is victorious, I will give the hidden manna. I will also give him a white stone inscribed with a new name, known only to the one who receives it." Revelations 2:17

(Rule) "…he who overcomes will be dressed in white. And I will never blot out his name from the Book of Life, but I will confess his name before My Father and His angels." Revelations 3:5

(Warning) "**I know all the things you do**, that you are neither hot nor cold. I wish that you were one or the other! But since you are like lukewarm water, neither hot nor cold, I will spit you out of my mouth!" Revelations 3:15,16

(Rule) "Behold, **I stand at the door and knock**. If anyone hears My voice and opens the door, I will come in and dine with him, and he with Me. To the one who is victorious, I will grant the right to sit with Me on My throne, just as I overcame and sat down with My Father on His throne." Revelations 3:20,21

(Warning) "Let the unrighteous continue to be unrighteous, and the vile continue to be vile; let the righteous continue to practice righteousness, and the holy continue to be holy." "Behold, I am coming quickly, and My reward is with Me, to give to each one according to what he has done. I am the Alpha and the Omega, the First and the Last, the Beginning and the End." Revelations 22:11-13

(Warning & Rule) "I testify to everyone who hears the words of prophecy in this book: If anyone adds to them, God will add to him the plagues described in this book. And if anyone takes away from the words of this book of prophecy, God will take away his share in the tree of life and in the holy city, which are described in this book." Revelations 22:18,19

To the Church on Elders, Overseers, Deacons and Good Ministers (church leaders)

(Instruction) "Not many of you should become teachers, my brothers, (Warning) because you know that **we who teach will be judged more strictly.**" James 3:1

(Instruction) "Obey your leaders and submit to them, (Warning) for **they watch over your souls as those who <u>must give an account</u>.**" Hebrew 13:17

(Instruction & Rule) "**An elder must** be blameless, the husband of but one wife, having children who are believers and are not open to accusation of indiscretion or insubordination." Titus 1:6

(Instruction & Rule) "**As God's steward, an overseer must** be above reproach—not self-absorbed, not quick-tempered, not given to drunkenness, not violent, not greedy for money." Titus 1:7

(Instruction & Rule) "If anyone aspires to be an overseer, he desires a noble task. **An overseer, then, must** be above reproach, the husband of but one wife, temperate, self-controlled, respectable, hospitable, able to teach, not dependent on wine, not violent but gentle, peaceable, and free of the love of money." 1 Timothy 3:1-3

(Instruction & Rule) "**An overseer must** manage his own household well and keep his children under control, with complete dignity. For if someone does not know how to manage his own household, how can he care for the church of God?" 1 Timothy 3:4,5

(Instruction & Rule) "**He must not** be a recent convert, or he may become conceited and fall under the same condemnation as the devil." 1 Timothy 3:6

(Instruction & Rule) "**...he must** have a good reputation with outsiders, so that he will not fall into disgrace and into the snare of the devil." 1 Timothy 3:7

(Instruction & Rule) "**He must** hold firmly to the trustworthy message as it was taught, so that by sound teaching he will be able to encourage others and refute those who contradict this message." Titus 1:9

(Instruction & Rule) "**Deacons likewise must** be dignified, not double-tongued or given to much wine or greedy for money." 1 Timothy 3,8

(Instruction & Rule) "**They must** hold to the mystery of the faith with a clear conscience." 1 Timothy 3:9

(Instruction & Rule) "Additionally, **they must** first be tested. Then, if they are above reproach, let them serve as deacons." 1 Timothy 3:10

(Instruction & Rule) "In the same way, **their wives must** be respected and must not slander others. They must exercise self-control and be faithful in everything they do." 1 Timothy 3:11

(Instruction & Rule) "**A deacon must** be the husband of but one wife, a good manager of his children and of his own household. For those who have served well as deacons acquire for themselves a high standing and great confidence in the faith that is in Christ Jesus." 1 Timothy 3:12,13

(Instruction & Rule) "I am writing you these things so that…you will know how each one must conduct himself in God's household, which is the church of the living God, the pillar and foundation of the truth." 1 Timothy 3:15

Good Ministers:

(Instruction) "…as for you, speak the things that are consistent with sound doctrine." Titus 2:1

(Warning) "Now **the Spirit expressly states** that in later times some will abandon the faith to follow deceitful spirits and the teachings of demons, influenced by the hypocrisy of liars…" 1 Timothy 4:1,2

(Instruction) "By pointing out these things to the brothers, you will be a good servant of Christ Jesus…" 1 Timothy 4:6

(Instruction) "…reject irreverent and silly myths. Instead, **train yourself for godliness.**" 1 Timothy 4:7

(Instruction) "…physical exercise is of limited value, but godliness is valuable in every way, holding promise for the present life and for the one to come. To this end we labor and strive, because **we have set our hope on the living God**, who is the Savior of all men, and especially of those who believe. **Command and teach these things.**" 1 Timothy 4:8,10,11

(Instruction) "…**set an example** for the believers in speech, in conduct, in love, in faith, in purity." 1 Timothy 4:12

(Instruction) "…**devote yourself** to the public reading of Scripture, to exhortation, and to teaching." 1 Timothy 4:13

(Instruction) "Do not neglect the gift that is in you…" 1 Timothy 4:14

(Instruction) "**Be diligent** in these matters and absorbed in them, so that your progress will be evident to all." 1 Timothy 4:15

(Instruction) "**Pay close attention** to your life and to your teaching."
1 Timothy 4:16

(Instruction) "**Persevere** in these things, for by so doing you will save
both yourself and those who hear you." 1 Timothy 4:16

(Instruction) "Do not rebuke an older man, but appeal to him as to a
father. Treat younger men as brothers, older women as mothers, and
younger women as sisters, with absolute purity." 1 Timothy 5:1,2

(Instruction) "**I solemnly charge you before God and Christ Jesus**
and the elect angels to maintain these principles without bias, and to
do nothing out of partiality." 1 Timothy 5:21

(Instruction) "Do not be too quick in the laying on of hands and
thereby share in the sins of others. **Keep yourself pure.**" 1 Timothy
5:22

(Instruction) "...**guard what has been entrusted to you**. Avoid irreverent, empty chatter and the opposing arguments of so-called "knowledge," which some have professed and thus swerved away from the
faith." 1 Timothy 6:20,21

(Instruction) "**Preach the word**; be prepared in season and out of
season; reprove, rebuke, and encourage with every form of patient
instruction. For the time will come when men will not tolerate sound
doctrine, but with itching ears they will gather around themselves
teachers to suit their own desires. So they will turn their ears away
from the truth and turn aside to myths. But you, be sober in all things,
endure hardship, do the work of an evangelist, fulfill your ministry."
2 Timothy 4:2-5

Policy for Good Ministers:

(Instruction) "**Give these instructions to the believers**, so that they will be above reproach. If anyone does not provide for his own, and especially his own household, he has denied the faith and is worse than an unbeliever." 1 Timothy 5:7,8

On widows:

(Instruction) "**Honor widows who are truly widows**. But if a widow has children, grandchildren or nephews (descendants), these should learn first of all to put their religion into practice at home by caring for their own family, for this is pleasing in the sight of God." 1 Timothy 5:3,4

(Instruction) "**The widow who is truly in need** and left all alone **puts her hope in God** and continues night and day in her petitions and prayers. But she who lives for pleasure is dead even while she is still alive." 1 Timothy 5:5,6

(Instruction) "**If any believing woman has dependent widows**, she must assist them and not allow the church to be burdened, so that it can help the widows who are truly in need." 1 Timothy 5:16

On widows brought into service in the church:

(Instruction) "…(only) if she is at least sixty years old, the wife of one man, and well known for good deeds such as bringing up children, hospitality to strangers, washing the feet of the saints, helped the afflicted, and devoting herself to every good work." 1 Timothy 5:9,10

(Instruction) "…refuse to enroll younger widows. For when their passions draw them away from Christ, they will want to marry, and thus will incur judgment because they are setting aside their first faith." 1 Timothy 5:11,12

On Elders:

(Instruction) "**Elders who lead effectively are worthy of double honor, especially those who work hard at preaching and teaching**. For the Scripture says, "Do not muzzle an ox while it is treading out the grain," and, "The worker is worthy of his wages." 1 Timothy 5:17,18

(Instruction) "Do not entertain an accusation against an elder, except on the testimony of two or three witnesses. But **those who persist in sin should be rebuked in front of everyone**, so that the others will stand in fear of sin." 1 Timothy 5:19,20

CHAPTER 9

The Diversity of Religions & Their Doctrines

After I had completed writing all but the final chapter, I was again reading Tozer and again found something that couldn't be left out: "Christian! Love Not the World." This 60-year-old instruction would have left us with quite different doctrines today had the Christians heeded it then.

> "It is the familiar world of sinful human society which swells about and beneath us as the waters of the flood once surged and churned around the ark of Noah. No Christian need fail to recognize it, provided he wants to know what it is and where it is located. Here are a few infallible marks of identification:

1. **Unbelief.** Wherever men refuse to come under the authority of the inspired Scriptures, there is the world. Religion without the Son of God is worldly religion. To have fellowship with those who live in unbelief is to love the world. The Christian's communion should be with Christians.

2. **Impenitence.** The people of the world will readily admit that they are sinners, but their lack of sorrow for sin distinguishes them from the children of God. The Christian mourns over his sin and is comforted. The worldling shrugs off his sin and continues in it.

3. **Godless philosophies.** Whether they know it or not, they who belong to the world live by a creed, and by their fruits we may know what their creed is. The man of the world, despite his protestations to the contrary, actually accepts the sufficiency of this world and makes no provision for any other; he esteems earth above heaven, time above eternity, body above soul and men above God. He holds sin to be relatively harmless, believes pleasure to be an end in itself, accepts the rightness of the customary and trusts to the basic

goodness of human nature. And even though he be an elder in a church he is part and parcel of the world.

4. **Externalism.** The man of heaven lives for the kingdom within him; the man of earth lives for the world around him. The first is born of the Spirit; the other is born of the flesh and will perish with it.

To sum up: whatever promotes self, cheapens life, starves the soul, hopes without biblical grounds for hope, adopts current moral standards, follows the way of the majority whether it be right or wrong, indulges in the pleasures of the flesh to make bearable the secret thoughts of death and judgment – that is the world.

'Love not the world, neither the things that are in the world. If any man love the world, the love of the Father is not in him' (1 John 2:15)."

I have not connected the following quotes with the churches from whose doctrines they are pulled, and have replaced any such reference within each quote with "specified denomination." This is only a partial list of doctrines pulled from a partial list of Christian denominations, although it should be clearly noted that "mainstream traditional denominations" are included in the referenced list. These include those I have had interactive relationships with and one that I attended for several years. Therefore, you should not assume this could not be your church. In fact, some of the great, godly men to whom these churches claim attachment would, as the saying goes, "turn over in their graves" if they knew what was being proclaimed in their names. I will say that, for the most part, locating the declared beliefs of particular denominations was quite the challenge. One would think that a Christian standing confidently, <u>Faithfully in the Truth of God</u>, should put those beliefs out for all the world to see and see easily. This begged the question: if they don't, what does that say? For me, it said they have something to hide. If a church holds beliefs contradictory to the Manual, move on. If a church hides their beliefs or makes them hard to find, catch that same bus… Move On. A quick note on that: Most will declare "Basic" beliefs on their front page and, as we've pointed out before, "even the demons believe that." In fact, it's the very question the demon asked the Seven Sons of Sceva, "Jesus I know, and I know about Paul, but who are you?" (Acts 19:15) We are again talking "application." How do they apply the Manual in teaching, in their church, and in life?

"Acknowledging as a justly influential motive His right to exact my obedience, there is the greater reason for carefully distinguishing what God in reality asserts, from what man would represent him to say." Robert Boyle

Note: As some of these doctrines have been adopted by several denominations and vary only slightly in their presentation, I only offer them once. Where informative, excerpts are pulled from more than one denomination resulting in multiple sections on certain topics (e.g. "On the Bible" is presented twice). Each quote is presented without alteration except when shortened, indicated by "…".

On the Bible: "Scripture, the saving revelation of God in Jesus Christ, addresses us with full divine authority in its total extent and in all its parts, and therefore the (specified denomination) speaks of the Bible as the inspired and infallible Word of God. The authority of Scripture is inseparable from the historical reality of the events recorded in it.

Interpreted historical events are presented in Scripture not simply as isolated events but for their revelational meaning. Scripture is self-authenticating; it is not dependent on the findings of science, but these findings may lead to a better understanding of Scripture and must be developed within a Christian community faithful to the authority of Scripture."

"Holy Scripture in its entirety is the written Word of God, inspired by God to be our rule of faith and practice. This inspiration is organic, extending to the ideas and the words of Scripture, and is so unique that Scripture alone is the Word of God. The human authors of Scripture were moved by the Holy Spirit so that their writing, reflecting their own personalities, language, and style, communicates infallibly God's self-revelation. Belief in the inspiration of Scripture, required by Scripture itself and by our Lord and his apostles, is indispensable to Christian faith. The infallibility of Scripture is inferred from inspiration, and the inspiration of Scripture secures its infallibility."

Let me say, I couldn't agree more with these doctrines. I just can't seem to wrap my head around a denomination that states boldly the previous and then, ignoring the same, jumps headlong into doctrines based on "man's wisdom" and man's Social/Secular Religion. You will see that, while great efforts are often made to link these "creature" doctrines to the Creator, when compared to the Instructions, Warnings and the Rules, they are revealed to be no more than lies of the Adversary.

On Stewardship of creation: "We uphold 'biblical principles of responsible dominion, care, and stewardship of creation,' recognizing that our continually growing knowledge about God's world should 'guide us in our love of God and neighbors, including care for the creation'; 'even when scientific uncertainties are taken into account,' we are compelled to address 'human-induced climate change' as 'an ethical, social justice, and religious issue'; we are therefore called to be 'voices for justice and public examples in the effort to live sustainably within our God-given resources, to promote stewardship in our own communities and our nations,' and to 'examine energy choices' in our daily life and work 'from a perspective of stewardship, challenging ourselves to use less energy and to use it more wisely' while seeking 'justice for the poor and vulnerable among us and for future generations.'"

On Justice: "The (specified denomination's) Office of Social Justice and Hunger Action is a ministry that deals with many social justice issues: restorative justice, racism, abortion, HIV/AIDS, poverty in North America, world hunger, war and peace, religious persecution, refugees, marginalization of immigrant workers, and more. In Canada, the (specified denomination's) Committee for Contact with the Government deals with similar advocacy issues. For more information, see...a report on restorative justice adopted by (specified denomination) 2005."

On Divorce: "The church must be a place of acceptance and support for those who have been divorced and for their children."

On Homosexuality: "Statements of pastoral advice: Homosexuality is a condition in which a person is sexually oriented toward persons of the same sex, and for which the person may bear only a minimal responsibility. Persons of same-sex attraction may not be denied community acceptance solely because of their sexual orientation and should be wholeheartedly received by the church and given loving support and encouragement. Same-sex oriented Christians, like all Christians, are called to discipleship, holy obedience, and the use of their gifts in the cause of the kingdom. Opportunities to serve within the offices and the life of the congregation should be afforded to same-sex oriented Christians as well as to heterosexual Christians."

On Creation: "All of life, including scientific endeavor, must be lived in obedience to God and in subjection to his Word. Therefore we encourage Christian scholarship that integrates faith and learning. The church does not impose an authorized interpretation of specific passages in Scripture; nor does it canonize certain scientific hypotheses. Instead, it insists that all theological interpretations and all scientific theories be subject to Scripture and the confessions.

Humanity is created in the image of God; all theorizing that minimizes this fact and all theories of evolution that deny the creative activity of God are rejected."

The previous is a great example of our earlier reference to the political approach to doctrine, "depends on what your definition of the word is, is." Here it is so well done it is as if it were straight from the Adversary's mouth, i.e. "humanity is created in the image of God" sounds good... until it goes off the rails with "The church does not impose an authorized interpretation of..." how God performed that "creation." Even though the "how" is clearly stated in Scripture and the same specified denomination's own doctrine first states: "The authority of Scripture is <u>inseparable from the historical reality of the events recorded in it</u>." And, "Holy Scripture <u>in its entirety</u> is the written Word of God, inspired by God to be our rule of faith and practice. This inspiration is organic, extending to the ideas and the words of Scripture, and is so unique that Scripture alone is the Word of God. The human authors of Scripture were moved by the Holy Spirit so that <u>their writing</u>, reflecting their own personalities, language, and style, <u>communicates infallibly God's self-revelation</u>. Belief in the inspiration of Scripture, required by Scripture itself and by our Lord and his apostles, is indispensable to Christian faith. The infallibility of Scripture is inferred from inspiration, and the inspiration of Scripture secures its infallibility."

Moving on:

On Repentance and Change: "We believe that God reaches out to the repentant believer in justifying grace with accepting and pardoning love. (Specified denomination) theology stresses that a decisive change in the human heart can and does occur under the prompting of grace and the guidance of the Holy Spirit."

In referencing the Old Testament and the Ten Commandments, i.e. the "Moral Law:" …no Christian whatsoever is free from obedience of the commandments which are called moral."

On the Church: "The visible church of Christ is a congregation of faithful men in which the pure word of God is preached…"

On the Bible (another denomination): "It is to be received through the Holy Spirit as the true rule and guide for faith and practice. Whatever is not revealed in or established by the Holy Scriptures is not to be made an article of faith nor is it to be taught as essential to salvation."

Again, we seem to have a church that firmly grounds itself in Biblical authority, yet…here we go again. Doctrines that reflect Social/Secular Political policies and even communist rhetoric rather than God's Word. Sadly this communist/socialist theme runs throughout these doctrines, so I will not supply all infected sections. (Have you read the "Communist Manifesto"? I have, including the draft letters written by Engles.)

On the sheepfold: "The services of worship of every local church of the (specified denomination) shall be open to all persons. The mark of an inclusive society is one in which all persons are open, welcoming, fully accepting, and supporting of all other persons, enabling them to participate fully in the life of the church, the community, and the world."

On Church Leadership: "Leadership is a gift from God, and can be expressed by all people in our church, regardless of sexual identity or orientation."

On Stewardship of creation: We encourage persons to limit CO_2 emissions toward the goal of one tonne per person annually. We strongly advocate for the priority of renewable energies. The deposits of carbon, oil, and gas resources are limited and their continuous utilization accelerates global warming. The use of nuclear power is no solution for avoiding CO_2 emissions."

NOTE, Published 2019: "This literary effort will present in layman's terms the proof that the primary definition of climate change, as viewed by the United Nations and expressed as caused by carbon dioxide (CO_2), is a myth. Therefore, the purported negative impacts on society by this cause are untrue – and that the continued promotion of this scientific fraud has caused financial losses to many and loss of life for some of our world's poorest inhabitants." Fleming, Rex J.. *The Rise and Fall of the Carbon Dioxide Theory of Climate Change*. Springer International Publishing.

Above all, Christians have a responsibility, not to mention an instruction from God, to pursue the Truth and to lead people and the church from that Truth. Those claiming the name of Christ should and must be above the political whims of an ungodly world.

"We acknowledge the global impact of humanity's disregard for God's creation. Rampant industrialization and the corresponding increase in the use of fossil fuels have led to a buildup of pollutants in the earth's atmosphere. These 'greenhouse gas' emissions threaten to alter dramatically the earth's climate for generations to come..."

On creation: "We find that science's descriptions of cosmological, geological and biological evolution are not in conflict with theology."

On abortion: "The beginning of life and the ending of life are the God-given boundaries of human existence. While individuals have always had some degree of control over when they would die, they now have the awesome power to determine when and even whether new individuals will be born. Our belief in the sanctity of unborn life makes us reluctant to approve abortion.

But....

Danger to the life of the mother. In the modern era, situations in which pregnancy seriously and imminently threatens the life of the mother are exceedingly rare. If, however, responsible diagnoses confirm that childbirth is likely to result in the death of the mother, historic Christian faith usually has favored the life of the mother above that of the unborn child. Unlike the unborn child, the mother is a mature person with established family and societal relationships and responsibilities."

In case you missed it, they essentially say, "We are 'reluctant' to usurp God's Sovereign Authority; 'if, however,' we lose Trust in Him and our Faith in His goodness and Providence is lacking, we are left with no choice..." In any interpretation of God's Instruction Manual I've read, there are no "buts" when it comes to God's Authority or our requirement for Faith. God not only died as Christ so that His children might live, He subjected Himself to prolonged torture and suffering on His children's behalf. The Manual also explicitly states that God is impartial and does not play favorites, that all human life is equal in value. Romans 2:11, "For there is no respect of persons (prosōpolēpsia) with God." Prosōpolēpsia "partiality, that is, favoritism" (Strong's) Also see Acts 10:34 and Deuteronomy 10:17. And yes, the Manual does speak specifically about our showing favoritism, "If you really keep the royal law stated in Scripture, "Love your neighbor as yourself," you are doing well. But if you show favoritism, you sin and are convicted by the law as transgressors." (James 2:8,9)

Only God knows all, so only God can know the potential impact of the baby on their family, society, "the Church" and the world. Even if true, such a doctrine is a stretching rationalization that weighs physical world value over the equality of God-given life. Furthermore, most of the world's greatest positive contributors were once "the unborn child" of average parents whose only significant contribution to the betterment of the world (in God's providence) was the birth of that child.

On Abortion: "Bearing children is a process of covenant-initiation that calls for courage, love, patience, and strength. In addition to these gifts of the Spirit, parent-child covenants also require the economic as well as the spiritual resources appropriate to the nurture of a human life. The magnitude of the commitment to be a human parent cannot be overestimated and should not be understated. The decision to terminate a pregnancy may be an affirmation of one's covenant responsibility to accept the limits of human resources. Because we understand the morality of abortion to be a question of stewardship of life, the responsible decision to choose abortion may arise from analysis of the projected resources for caregiving in a specific situation.

Abortion can therefore be considered a responsible choice within a Christian ethical framework when serious genetic problems arise or when the resources are not adequate to care for a child appropriately. Elective abortion, when responsibly used, is intervention in the process of pregnancy precisely because of the seriousness with which one regards the covenantal responsibility of parenting."

The ridiculousness and utter lack of Scriptural grounding speaks for itself with this one. So let me just provide the denominations who hold this theology with a link where they can educate themselves on a new thing: https://adoption.org/ OK... maybe not so new. After all, Moses was adopted when his birth mother found, after an "analysis" of her "specific situation," that the "limits of human resources" in her life were "not adequate to care for a child appropriately." What Christian isn't glad she chose adoption over death?

On "Right to" a job: "Every person has the right to a job at a living wage. Where the private sector cannot or does not provide jobs for all who seek and need them, it is the responsibility of government to provide for the creation of such jobs."

On church and state: "We believe that the state should not attempt to control the church, nor should the church seek to dominate the state. The rightful and vital separation of church and state, which has served the cause of religious liberty..."

"(specified denomination) contend that this mutual benefit works best when the institutions of church and state are separate and when neither seeks to control the other."

Any individual "church" or denomination that believes that you can achieve Moral Clarity, Righteous Judgement and True Justice "separate" from God takes on His Authority and He "takes no pleasure in them." A person or denomination who claims to be part of Christ's "sheepfold" but praises "Separation of Church and State" as it has been applied since the Supreme Court's first opinion on the matter shows not only a lack of historical knowledge of the issue but of the country itself.

"Under God" was added to "One nation, indivisible..." in the Pledge of Allegiance in 1954, and the social/secular world has sought to paint it as a modern-day effort to inject God into America and rewrite history. However, "indivisible" has been part of the Pledge since the first version (1892). On June 16th, 1858, Abraham Lincoln gave a speech containing the reference, "A house divided against itself, cannot stand." Both "indivisible" and Lincoln's quote were references to a quote from Christ Himself, "How can Satan drive out Satan? If a kingdom is divided against itself, it cannot stand." (Mark 3:23,24)

A very quick historical summary of "The Wall of Separation:"

A small Christian church in Connecticut, The Danbury Baptist, wrote a letter to Thomas Jefferson concerned that the "free exercise" clause of the Constitution was a step away from the statement, "endowed by their Creator with certain unalienable Rights" written in The Declaration of Independence a few years earlier. They were concerned that this new statement would allow the government to declare a particular denomination within the Christian church as a "National Religion," as had been the case in Britain from which they had declared their Independence. Jefferson assured the men that the "whole American people" had prohibited such a practice and that this new amendment was to bind the legislature not only from attempting to do so but from interfering or injecting themselves into the Church, as a group or as an individual, at all. Although Jefferson's letter references the documents adopted by "the whole American people," his letter was not one of them. In a masterful act of the Adversary, the personal opinion of one President provided to re-assure the Church that the government was forever bound from taking on the "Creator's" Authority was grasped onto by the courts overstepping their legal restrictions and canonizing the opposite position into law.

As the doctrines show, some modern-day denominations have abandoned their loyalty to Christ and, instead of declaring our Endowment, trumpet the positions of Social/Secular Religion, including that the "Creator" who "Endowed" our rights should no longer have a say in their protection.

On "same-sex" relationships: "(Specified denomination) called upon congregations and members to welcome, care for, and support same-gender couples and their families and to advocate for their legal protection."

This denomination says that after many years of "faithful study" they have not come to a consensus on what the Manual Instructs on this issue. How long did it take you to read the previous chapter? How long did it take you to read the Instructions on this issue? Do you think they are undecided about "Thieves," "Drunkards" or "Abusers" as are also warned against in 1 Corinthians 6? So, why do they "Let this instruction go"? When Galatians 5 says, "The acts of the flesh are <u>obvious</u>…" what are they having trouble understanding? What's confusing about, "<u>Put to death</u>, therefore, the components of your earthly nature: <u>sexual immorality, impurity, lust</u>, evil desires, and greed…"? (Colossians 3) (from another denomination) "We do not have agreement on whether this church should honor these relationships and uplift, shelter, and protect them or on precisely how it is appropriate to do so."

In contrast to the previous, I provide this quote which I had put on a canvas and now hangs in our worship room: "Worship is no longer worship when it reflects the culture around us more than the Christ within us." A.W. Tozer

Let me ask you, do these doctrines reflect Christ's **Instructions, Warnings and Rules**, or did they sound more like the United Nations' handbook? Remember, these are only examples of blatant secularism and disregard for our Creator pulled from the many pages of many church doctrines. I couldn't bring myself to add the several references that directly point to and promoted the UN and its policies, not to mention cheerleading membership to this worldly organization. "…we endorse the United Nations, its related bodies…We urge acceptance for membership in the United Nations…" If Social/Secular Religion had a central church, the UN would be it.

To close this chapter, I wanted to include this doctrine and show it at the end because, after reading the doctrines of several denominations, I thought my head would explode. As they say on TV, I felt like I needed a bath. I hold this doctrine out because it is the proverbial "bar of soup" in that analogy. I literally read page after page after page… after page, of many denominations going to great lengths to justify, support, and advocate for various ways of discrimination. We just quoted Romans 2:11 that clearly says God does not justify, support or advocate for "playing favorites," yet these churches "pick out what they like and let the rest go." To them, I say, if God is no "respecter of persons," if even He does not find a reason to show "favoritism," then who are you? Who are you to advocate the preference of one of God's creations over another through "Affirmative Action?" Who are you to lobby the legislated theft from those you declare wealthy to give to those you declare poor? God sees us all the same. We do not correct man's failures by adopting those same failures and renaming them "Social Justice." We adopt and Live In God's Truth. We become Color Blind and Gender Blind, we don't simply switch the prejudice. Or, as a man who actually knew prejudice said, we "judge a man by the content of their character..." not worldly or superficial standards. (If I have to tell you that was MLK, well then... that's just sad)

As I said at the beginning of this chapter, far too much of what I read sounded... no, not sounded, could have been taken directly from the Communist Manifesto or the campaign ads of one of the Socialists running for President. Also, as I said, don't assume these couldn't be your church... the worst offender reviewed was once mine. So, here is what a representative of God, Christ, and the Holy Spirit should sound like on the issue:

Equal Rights. "The (specified denomination) upholds the right of all individuals to equal opportunity politically, economically, and religiously, and pledges itself to an active effort to bring about the possession of dignity and happiness by all people everywhere." (underlines are mine)

Ahhh... I am so glad I didn't come across this one until the end of my research!

I can't think of better "bookends" than to begin a chapter with Tozer and end it with Boyle:

"Not only do far fewer religions differ fundamentally than men perceive, but far fewer men follow any of those religions of their own choice than some believe. For it is one thing for a man to profess this or that religion, but another thing entirely for him to choose the best. For the latter cannot be done save by one who has seriously and carefully examined the religion he has embraced in preference to others, and has compared it with them. But unless this serious and deliberate choice has taken place, one cannot legitimately conclude from the number of men adhering to that religion that it is the best... Thus, when all things are duly considered, we may readily note that there are few who choose a given religion, even though there are many who follow it, for the rest all behave passively, so to speak, each man professing his religion more by chance than by judicious choice." Robert Boyle's unpublished treatise "On the Diversity of Religions."

Included at the end of the Resource section in the back of this book is a list of web addresses (links) to doctrines published online by various denominations. What I would like you to know about this list is:

Everything included in this chapter comes from a source on this list although not everyone on the list has been quoted. However, just because they are on the list does not indicate they are good or bad, as the final quoted doctrine shows. Also, as stated at the beginning of the chapter, this is only a partial compilation of quotes from the list. It is worth repeating that if more than one denomination held a virtually indistinguishable position, only one quote was included to represent all. Therefore, it would not be fair to point out which was used as the example. It would also be justly unreasonable to print them all. This list is not, nor could it be, comprehensive. There were those I researched whose political structure made it very difficult to track doctrines and those whose doctrines I could not locate before moving on.

That said, it is not my responsibility to survey the sheepfold you are considering… it is yours. I will, however, give you a couple of tips. In my research, it remained consistent that the more words it took to state or justify a position the further away from God's it moved. Those who took the Manual at its Word were short and direct with no need to sell. You should also consider the proposed fold at a more intimate level. Meaning, the denominational level is not necessarily representative of the individual church. This adds to the scrutiny you must have in searching for the Truth. For example, as already noted, one of the worst offenders was one I attended. Long before the denomination arrived where they are today, I sat and listened to our church representatives' reports upon their return from the national conference. They expressed their grief and concern that activists were pushing for doctrines to move away from Scripture and towards the world, towards the doctrines they proudly hold today. While this discrepancy can run in either direction, here's the problem with this one. The individual church did not hold the unscriptural positions the denomination to which they belonged did… and therein is the problem. From all appearances that local fold seemed safe, seemed to be a Sanctuary. But, the denomination to which they belonged clearly wasn't. Proof they were not the safe place they appeared to be? Today it is still <u>the denomination to which they belong</u>, the denomination their funds support, the denomination whose doctrines are represented by the sign out front, the denomination led by false prophets, false teachers and heretics.

I have also seen the issue run in the other direction. I have experienced members of local folds and colleges holding and teaching positions far outside of the stated doctrines of the denomination to which they belong. Sadly, the denomination had wandered away from Scriptural Truth, and those down the ladder adopted their move to man's authority over God's and ran with it.

The point being, even if you found a denomination with a committed Scriptural doctrine, you should not assume the local fold upholds it. Vice versa, just because a local fold appears to be safe, you should not assume they are. If they belong to, support or turn a blind eye to a denomination that takes God's authority upon themselves, then beware of the wolves... and move on.

Don't be discouraged, you are not the only sheep, and God's appointed shepherds and teachers are out there. In their presence, the wolf, the goat and the lion have no power.

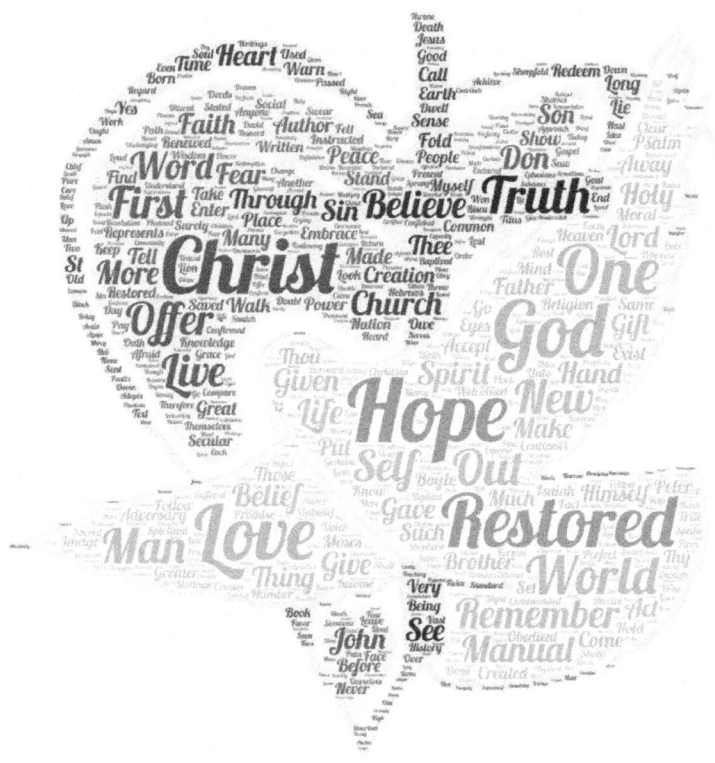

CHAPTER 10

Restored Hope & The Guarantee

"I owe all that I am to Him who made me: but how can I pay my debt to Him who redeemed me, and in such wondrous wise? Creation was not so vast a work as redemption; for it is written of man and of all things that were made, 'He spake the word, and they were made' (Psalm 148.5). But to redeem that creation which sprang into being at His word, how much He spake, what wonders He wrought, what hardships He endured, what shames He suffered! Therefore what reward shall I give unto the Lord for all the benefits which He hath done unto me? In the first creation He gave me myself; but in His new creation He gave me Himself, and by that gift restored to me the self that I had lost. Created first and then restored, I owe Him myself twice over in return for myself. But what have I to offer Him for the gift of Himself? Could I multiply myself a thousand-fold and then give Him all, what would that be in comparison with God?"

This is how St. Bernard of Clairvaux described **The Offer of Hope** in *On Loving God*. This is the Hope we have forgotten. First, that we were created by the hand and voice of God. But then, before He uttered the words, "Let Us make man in Our image," He had already planned a gift for us. This gift, that could only come from His Grace, was a restoration to the image in which we were created, empowered by the indwelling of the Holy Spirit of God Himself. This new creation can only be achieved by embracing the **Hope** that is Christ. Christ – God born a man… Christ – persecuted, tortured and killed at the hands of His fellow man… Christ – resurrected, risen and sitting (present tense) at the right hand of God. By standing and walking firmly, confidently in this **Truth,** we show Faith; from this **Faith,** we find Favor in the eyes of God; from this **Grace,** we are welcomed through the "Narrow Gate" into the Spiritual World of our Creator.

Bernard continues:

"He is all that I need, all that I long for. (Psalm 18) My God and my help, I will love Thee for Thy great goodness; not so much as I might, surely, but as much as I can. I cannot love Thee as Thou deservest to be loved, for I cannot love Thee more than my own feebleness permits. I will love Thee more when Thou deemest me worthy to receive greater capacity for loving; yet never so perfectly as Thou hast deserved of me. 'Thine eyes did see my substance, yet being unperfect; and in Thy book all my members were written' (Psalm 139:16). Yet Thou recordest in that book all who do what they can, even though they cannot do what they ought. Surely I have said enough to show how God should be loved and why. But who has felt, who can know, who express, how much we should love him."

It is through living in this knowledge that we gain wisdom, and it is through this wisdom that we achieve Peace. A Peace that doesn't just know but understands, "What Can Man Do To Me?!" This Peace knows that God's Love overcomes all the Physical World can throw at His people. **Christ,** our **Hope,** says, "I offer you Peace that your heart will not be troubled and that you will not be afraid." So, we face the Adversary's world and we are not afraid. We Embrace the Manual, follow its Instructions, keep Christ's commandments and Love as God Loves.

The promise:

"Then I saw a new heaven and a new earth, for the first heaven and earth had passed away, and the sea was no more…I heard a loud voice from the throne saying: 'Behold, the dwelling place of God is with man, and He will dwell with them. They will be His people, and God Himself will be with them as their God. He will wipe away every tear from their eyes, and there will be no more death or mourning or crying or pain, for the former things have passed away." (Revelations 21:1,3,4)

First Believe in The Author

Common sense and life in general tell us that if you don't believe in the source of something, you won't truly believe in what comes from it. The Manual tells us the same thing about anyone who would reach for **The Offer**, who would approach God: "...anyone who approaches Him must believe that He exists." This belief is not merely in the concept of God but in God as He represents and documents Himself through the writings of Moses, Isaiah, David, Paul and the rest who immortalized His stated Truth through the Manual – Old and New. I love the imagery that Boyle used representing this Truth drawn from Matthew 17:3: "I sometimes contemplate Moses and Elias talking with Christ — I mean the law and the prophets harmonizing with the Gospel." That is the requirement. We must believe that God is who He says He is and that He gives us that knowledge through the writings of Moses, the Prophets, and the Apostles. Again from Boyle, "I would compare Scripture, in regard to its expressions, to a rose, in which so great a number of leaves so nearly resemble each, other, but there is not one contained in the flower, that does not contribute to its perfection and beauty." And "...knowing that some persons are to be wrought upon by reason, others allured by interest; some impelled by terror, others again enticed by example; the Supreme Author, by an incomprehensible suppleness of wisdom, so varied the heavenly doctrine into ratiocinations (reasoning), mysteries, promises, threats, and examples; that under whatever circumstances the devout reader may be placed, he will find religion represented in that form, by which he is most likely to be pleased and captivated."

Boyle also proposes Truths regarding failure to do the previous: "unbelief is productive of more sins than we are accustomed to impute to it: and that many persons who are baptized into the Christian faith are not exempt." There may be no one Truth more represented in the history of man: Doubt in the Author. This Truth can be traced from the very first doubt acted on by Adam to many of the doctrines of many of the churches representing Christ today. These "Christians" embrace the beliefs of the Adversary's world, dismiss Moses, and question the written Word of God, confirming another of Boyle's beliefs: "I am confirmed in the belief, that by transferring our impressions to the Sacred Text, we often impute to the Scriptures our own faults and deficiencies." Those who do such things take the Author's Authority on themselves and are a threat to the entire "sheepfold." We must believe that He exists. This is not optional or negotiable. Yes, He "knocks," but, before we can accept His invitation, we must accept every word of Who He says He is. After all, to call God a liar is to reject The Offer.

"The One who comes from heaven is above all. He testifies to what He has seen and heard, yet no one accepts His testimony. Whoever accepts His testimony has certified that God is truthful. For the One whom God has sent speaks the words of God…" John 3:31-34

"See to it, brothers, that none of you has a wicked heart of unbelief that turns away from the living God…to whom did He swear that they would never enter His rest? Was it not to those who disobeyed? So we see that it was because of their unbelief that they were unable to enter." Hebrews 3:12,18,19

Live in Hope

This is the requirement of **The Offer** that we must remember. In order to receive the **Hope** Christ offers, we must "Live in that Hope." As Christ welcomes us into His "sheepfold," we are to "…put on the

new self, created to be like God in true righteousness and holiness."
(Ephesians 4:24) The Manual is clear that this "New Self" is not an
external act or change in behavior but an internal one that is manifest
externally: "…be renewed in the spirit of your minds." (Ephesians 4:23)
And "…put on the new self, which is being renewed in knowledge in
the image of its Creator." (Colossians 3:10) Titus 3:5 represents what
is stated repeatedly in the Manual, "He saved us, not by the righteous
deeds we had done, but according to His mercy, through the washing
of <u>new birth and renewal</u> by the Holy Spirit." The Manual is also clear
on what that "new birth and renewal" look like: "As obedient children,
do not conform to the passions of your former ignorance." (1Peter
1:14) And "Do not love the world or anything in the world. If anyone
loves the world, the love of the Father is not in him." (1 John 2:15) Or,
as Havner put it, "If you are what you've always been, you are not a
Christian. A Christian is a new creation." The idea too many of today's
churches perpetuate is that you can retain the thoughts as long as you
don't perform the "acts" from those thoughts. This is absolutely contrary to the Manual and Christ's instruction to "The Church." "Let the
words of my mouth, <u>and the meditation of my heart</u>, be acceptable in
thy sight, O LORD, my strength, and my redeemer." (Psalm 19:14) "…
clothe yourselves with the Lord Jesus Christ, and make no provision
for the desires of the flesh." (Romans 13:14)

As Christ is our Hope, the Chief Shepherd (John 10:11) warns His
flock not to be lured away from our Hope by such teachers: "…do not
be foolish, but understand what the Lord's will is." "Test and prove
what pleases the Lord. <u>Have no fellowship</u> with the fruitless deeds of
darkness, but rather expose them." (Ephesians 5:17, 5:10,11) In fact,
the Manual says that if we look to the Father, if we first believe that He
exists and live in that belief, our Hope is secure. "I give them eternal

life, and they will never perish. No one can snatch them out of My hand. My Father who has given them to Me is greater than all. No one can snatch them out of My Father's hand. I and the Father are one." (John 10:28-30) And because our Hope is secure, we can live in Peace, as citizens of the Spiritual World and "strangers" (1 Peter 2:11) in, but not "of," the Physical World.

Common sense should tell us that if this is the standard we are to hold individually, then this is the standard we are to hold when we, as individuals, gather together in a community, i.e. "The Church." But, in case our common sense is lacking, we showed in chapter 4, "The Church," what the first church looked like and how we are instructed to follow that example.

They were All Believers

They had Everything in Common

They were of One Accord

They Devoted Themselves to the Apostles' Teaching

They were Saved

Havner said this about the impact of those who do not hold to these standards, "When the Lord's white sheep become dirty gray, all black sheep feel more comfortable." The good news is this: if we as sheep view ourselves as Sanctuaries, living lives that put "self" where it belongs; if we make our hearts a "Sacred Place;" if we live lives of "Reverence" to God, The Shepherd, and The Spirit; then we ourselves will walk into that church as "a House Consecrated to the Worship of God." As such, we will recognize our fellow sheep. We will reject a fold where goats, wolves and hirelings are present. Our cups will be cleaned from the inside out, and the world will see our Shepherd in us. When we find a fold free of the Adversary's agents in wool, a place of true worship, we will be strengthened by the flock and its Great Shepherd. From this place of Spiritual Power, we are given a task: to "go out" from that community and relay **The Offer of Hope** to others. This is known as **"The Great Commission."** "Go into all the world and preach the gospel to every creature. Whoever believes and is baptized will be saved, but whoever does not believe will be condemned." (Mark 16:15,16) "Then Jesus came to them and said, "All authority in heaven and on earth has been given to Me. Therefore, go and make disciples of all nations, baptizing them in the name of the Father, and of the Son, and of the Holy Spirit, and teaching them to obey all that I have commanded you. And surely I am with you always, to the very end of the age." (Matthew 28:18-20)

If you have listened to very many of Tozer's sermons you would have heard him remark about the wolf or the goat that would wander into his church. Tozer said he wasn't particularly concerned about either because they would not be there long. He was expressing what we talk about regarding a Sanctuary. We said if we make ourselves a house consecrated to the worship of God, then when we walked into a church claiming to be a sheepfold we would recognize it for what it was. If it was a sincere fold, we would feel the Spirit's presence and kinship with our fellow sheep and we would be comfortable remaining. If not, we would recognize it as a den rather than a fold and we would leave. Tozer's point is rooted in the same Truth. He said that should a wolf or a goat find themselves in his church, in his fold's Santuary, they would soon recognize it for what it was. They would not feel comfortable and they would leave. It may have taken one sermon or at most a couple and the spirit they embraced would begin to squirm and itch and grumble at the Truths presented and they would leave.

Tozer would also make clear that this reaction was not because they were not treated well or in a welcoming manner, as he would relate that his members epitomized both. The truth was, while all were treated with welcoming hearts, All were Not Welcome. Because Tozer and his flock held firmly to the Truth, All felt judged and, in that environment, only the sheep, found and lost, would remain. All others would flee into the darkness, into the arms of their father, the father of lies… The Adversary.

The Guarantee

"…the **hope** of eternal life, which God, who cannot lie, promised before time began." Titus1:2

"God is not a man, that He should lie, or a son of man, that He should change His mind." Numbers 23:19

"…**hope** does not disappoint us, because God has poured out His love into our hearts through the Holy Spirit, whom He has given us." Romans 5:5

"Men swear by someone greater than themselves, and their oath serves as a confirmation to end all argument. So when God wanted to make the unchanging nature of His purpose very clear to the heirs of the promise, He guaranteed it with an oath (by Himself as there is no one greater, Heb 6:13). Thus, by two unchangeable things in which it is impossible for God to lie, we who have fled to take hold of the **hope** set before us may be strongly encouraged.

We have this **hope** as an anchor for the soul, firm and steadfast. It enters the inner sanctuary behind the curtain, where Jesus our forerunner has entered on our behalf. He has become a high priest forever..."
Hebrews 6:16-20

God's Love and Our Vigilance

Strong's says the words used for God's Love are "agapē" and "agapaō." In reading both the definitions and the references we provided this definition for what <u>Love Is: "Genuine affection for another by a deliberate act of will, in moral clarity, as a matter of principle."</u> As Christians, we are instructed to Love as God loves. What's that look like? "God so Loved the world He gave His one and only Son..." (John 3:16) Let's think about that for a second. God's Love for you meant He gave His one and only Son, not just for the big finish, but to leave His Kingdom, His seat at His Father's right hand, and be born a human. Not just to become a human, but to suffer persecution and torture at the hands of the creatures He came to save. But this Love was not just a sacrifice of the Father, it was a partnership with the Son. The Father gave His Son, but the Son came, the Son suffered, the Son did not fear, the Son did not run or use His unlimited power against His created man. The Son said, "I am the good shepherd. The good shepherd lays down His life for the sheep." (John 10:11) Why is that? "There is no fear in love, but perfect love drives out fear..." (1 John 4:18)

Today, many have "taken the parts of God's instruction on Love they like and let the rest go." Their love is not God's Love. It exists in a judgement-free zone, a God-free zone. While they may think they are getting away with their "alternate versions" now, the Truth will ultimately be revealed. "...all the churches will know that I am the One who searches minds and hearts, and I will repay each of you according to your deeds." (Revelations 2:23). "The LORD is slow to anger, abounding in Love and forgiving sin and rebellion. Yet He does not leave the guilty unpunished" (Numbers 14:18). These are only two examples where God warns that His Love cannot be separated from His Truth.

The Manual also teaches, "For God has not given us a spirit of timidity, but of power, Love, and self-control." (2 Timothy 1:7) God's Love teaches us to "Avoid the fire," He instructs, "Don't do these things," and "Don't put a 'stumbling block' in front of your neighbor. Love them enough to warn them also." Contrary to modern teachings, God's Love does not make us weak or tolerant of sin, just the opposite! True Love gives us the power to stand up to sin with Moral Clarity and, with Genuine Affection, fight for our brother as a Deliberate Act of Will. Love is born in "Divine Truth." God says that we can only truly "Love" our brother once we have "walked in that Truth." "Since you have purified your souls by obedience to the truth, so that you have a genuine Love for your brothers, Love one another deeply, from a pure heart." (1 Peter 1:22)

Love for God Is: obedience to His commandments, "Faith in Truth." **Love for our brother Is:** having no fear, "obedience to the Truth" and expecting the same.

History shows that we are on the very path predicted in the Manual. Mankind has become arrogant and, from their imaginations, has built their own religion based on their own worldliness. This new Social/ Secular Religion is in fact not new but raises its serpent-like head every time a nation becomes rich, powerful, and self-centered. This man-made religion replaces the Morality prescribed by God with a self-serving Secular Morality.

"I said, 'Here I am! Here I am!' to a nation that did not call My name. All day long I have held out My hands to an obstinate people, who walk in the wrong path, who follow their own imaginations, to a people who continually provoke Me to My face...They say, 'Keep to yourself; do not come near me, for I am holier than you!'" Isaiah 65:1-3,5

History has also shown that every time a nation adopts this Social/Secular Religion it is unknowingly in its "death throes." As Christians, we are warned, "Be vigilant and sober-minded. Your adversary the devil prowls around like a roaring lion, seeking someone to devour. Resist him, standing firm in your faith and in the knowledge that your brothers throughout the world are undergoing the same kinds of suffering." (1 Peter 5:8,9) Sadly, many denominations do not heed the warning and have adopted the beliefs of this Social/Secular Religion as their own. They have torn down the walls of the "sheepfold" and welcomed all – sheep, wolf, goat, and lion alike.

Isaiah 65 continues, "...you who forsake the LORD, who forget My holy mountain, who set a table for Fortune and fill bowls of mixed wine for Destiny, I will destine you for the sword, and you will all kneel down to be slaughtered, because I called and you did not answer, I spoke and you did not listen; you did evil in My sight and chose that in which I did not delight." (v:11,12)

Yes, God offers **Christ**. God offers **Hope**, but we must be vigilant to guard it for the day when we can redeem it for our Salvation. Our Adversary has successfully poisoned the World, and the churches are not immune. We must take care and, with "Sober Minds," compare the beliefs, the morals, they stand on, with those given by God in His Love. We must compare their doctrine to God's Revelation and, if they don't match, embrace our Manual and move on.

Before I Say Goodbye...

By "goodbye" I mean, "until we meet again," and by meet again I mean book 2 in the Hope Series – I want to make a final statement to the Lost. We have talked about the Manual and the Instructions and Warnings contained within it. We also showed that while immorality is immorality, wherever you stand, these were given for the believer to uphold; an unbeliever's fate is to join the Adversary regardless.

However, this is another area where the Adversary's whispers have twisted the Truth in an attempt to hide The Offer of Hope. No unbelieving sheep is too bad or too lost to be found by the Great Shepherd. Who you were or what you did yesterday does not matter. That is the "old self." It is this distinction between the old self and the New Self, as James and Havner just referenced, that sets the rules for the game. An unbeliever may have been divorced thirty-five times; they are no more condemned than the person married once for thirty-five years who attends church every Sunday and gives half their income to charity but, like Agrippa, only believes in 98% of who God says He is. If these two people were to go to church on the same day and kneel beside each other declaring their complete belief in the Triune One and embracing Hope, they would both be standing in the same place with the same clean slate. From that point, both are accountable for their doubts and their acts against God's "commandments and judgments." If either were to divorce and re-marry tomorrow, they would be held no less or more accountable than the other (Matthew 19:8,9). And if the one refused to warn the other of this stumbling block, they would be held accountable for their failure.

So, no, "All" are not "Welcome" through the door, but All Are Invited. If you set your baggage down, leave it behind and reach for Christ's outstretched hands, He will Welcome You into His Father's Fold and you will spend eternity in peace and rest. Until that day of entrance into eternity, no longer Lost, you must respect the fold, honor the Sanctuary and "Go Out" among the goats and the wolves, bringing the invitation, The Offer, to other Lost Sheep. Until the day when all are found and returned home. Until the day Christ returns.

Allow me to close borrowing from Tozer:

> "What, then, are we to do? Each one of us must decide, and there are at least three possible choices. One is to rise up in shocked indignation and accuse me of irresponsible reporting. Another is to nod general agreement with what is written here but take comfort in the fact that there are exceptions and we are among the exceptions. The other is to go down in meek humility and confess that we have grieved the Spirit and dishonored our Lord in failing to give Him the place His Father has given Him as Head and Lord of the Church.
>
> Either the first or the second will but confirm the wrong. The third if carried out to its conclusion can remove the curse. The decision lies with us."
>
> "He knocks" and He awaits our answer...

The Biographies

A. W. Tozer (1897 – 1963) Born a farm boy in Pennsylvania, Tozer was educated by the will of others only until the sixth grade. However, at the age of seventeen, Tozer heard The Call through the voice of a German street preacher. He answered that call kneeling alone in his attic that same night. Tozer himself would tell you he was not a saint overnight; in fact, the next couple of years had some rough patches. But God had created Tozer for something more. As he would later find out when he joined the military, his IQ was in the top four percent. With that, God took over where man had left off. There may have been no one with a greater thirst for written knowledge than Tozer. He never went to seminary, relying instead on this thirst and the Holy Spirit to teach him. Obviously, this informal education served him and God well as he was in great demand to speak to both church and student bodies at the very schools he never attended.

Tozer recounts finding a solitary place in a nearby woods after his ordination ceremony. In this account, he records his conversation with God to the best of his recollection. From the **"Prayer of a Minor Prophet"** we read Tozer's view of his qualifications and his appointment:

> "My God, I shall not waste time deploring my weakness nor my unfittedness for the work. The responsibility is not mine, but Thine. Thou hast said, **"I knew thee – I ordained thee – I sanctified thee,"** and Thou hast also said, "Thou shalt go to all that I shall send thee, and whatsoever I command thee thou shalt speak." Who am I to argue with Thee or to call into question Thy sovereign

choice? The decision is not mine but Thine. So be it, Lord. Thy will, not mine, be done."

"It is time, O God, for Thee to work, for the enemy has entered into Thy pastures and the sheep are torn and scattered. And false shepherds abound who deny the danger and laugh at the perils which surround Thy flock. The sheep are deceived by these hirelings and follow them with touching loyalty while the wolf closes in to kill and destroy. I beseech Thee, give me sharp eyes to detect the presence of the enemy; give me understanding to see and courage to report what I see faithfully. Make my voice so like Thine own that even the sick sheep will recognize it and follow Thee."

Having listened to and read as much of Tozer as I can get my hands on, I find it beyond me to identify an area that escaped his self-taught knowledge. Tozer possessed an understanding that spanned from Aristotle and Plato to Arminius and Calvin and far beyond. He said in his sermons that he would get the latest Bible translations as soon as they came out. This did not mean, however, that he accepted them all; some quickly retired to his library shelves. I'm also not sure there was a hymn he couldn't quote. Yes, I mean quote as he also often said, "You wouldn't want to hear me sing."

What Tozer discussed with God in that quiet woods turned out to be 100%. While growing the Christian and Missionary Alliance church in Chicago from 80 to 800 members, he also spoke around the continent, wrote books, could be heard on the radio and was editor of the *Alliance Weekly* Magazine from 1950 until his death in 1963. His first editorial from June 3rd, 1950, "Quality vs Quantity" showed his "courage to report" bluntly:

> "It will cost something to walk slow in the parade of the ages, while excited men of time rush about confusing motion with progress. But it will pay in the long run and the true Christian is not much interested in anything short of that."

And we see it still present in his last editorial printed 3 days after his death:

> "My relations with my own church as well as with Christians of other denominations have been friendly, courteous and pleasant. My grief is simply the result of a condition which I believe to be almost universally prev-alent among the churches... Let me state the cause of my burden. It is this: Jesus Christ has today almost no authority at all among the groups that call themselves by His name... By these I mean not the Roman Catholics nor the liberals, nor the various quasi-Christian cults. I do mean Protestant churches generally, and I include those that protest the loudest that they are in spiritual descent from our Lord and His apostles, namely, the evangeli-cals... Among the gospel churches Christ is now in fact little more than a beloved symbol. 'All Hail the Power of Jesus' Name' is the church's national anthem and the cross is her official flag, but in the week-by-week services of the church and the day-by-day conduct of her members someone else, not Christ, makes the decisions"

He closes the article with:

> "What, then, are we to do? Each one of us must decide, and there are at least three possible choices. One is to rise up in shocked indignation and accuse me of irresponsible reporting. Another is to nod general agreement with what is written here but take comfort in the fact that there are exceptions and we are among the exceptions. The other is to go down in meek humility and confess that we have grieved the Spirit and dishonored our Lord in failing to give Him the place His Father has given Him as Head and Lord of the Church.
>
> Either the first or the second will but confirm the wrong. The third if carried out to its conclusion can remove the curse. The decision lies with us."

I think these first and last prophetic editorials sum Tozer up. I don't think it a coincidence that God snatched a young A.W. Tozer off the street when He did or that he put the words in his mouth that He did. At a time when the world was about to remove prayer from school, legalize abortion, make divorce easier and much, much more, God sent a man to tell the churches, "You are lost in the darkness and the darkness grows. You have left 'The Church' and joined the world. Turn around and rejoin the flock before it's too late!"

David M'Clure, Doctor of Divinity (1748 – 1820) Of Scottish descent, David M'Clure was a preacher and teacher whose grandfather emigrated from "the north of Ireland." M'Clure was one of twelve children. Having "read the Bible through when (he) was very young," his father fostered David's love for books and sent him to "Latin Grammar School." David said he "desired an education to qualify (him) for usefulness," so, he left home at the age of fifteen to pursue greater learning. After an education at the Moore's school, M'Clure went on to graduate from then Yale College where his Valedictory speech "Defended a Latin Syllogistic Thesis." According to M'Clure's diary, "About this time, the Colonies came into a non-importation agreement on goods from Great Britain in consequence of the Stamp Act & other arbitrary acts of the British parliament. The Class agreed with 3 or 4 dissensients, to appear in home made clothes at the Commencement. We were put to some difficulty to obtain all the articles of American manufacture. Inspired with a patriotic spirit, we took pride in our plain coarse republican dress, & were applauded by the friends of Liberty." Following this, M'Clure returned to run the Moore's school that had so benefited him. M'Clure spent his life teaching either from the pulpit or in the classroom. In 1777, he became a trustee at Dartmouth College and later was awarded the honorary degree of Doctor of Divinity. He was pastor of the Church of East Windsor, Conn. for thirty-four years. In "Sprague's Annals of the American Pulpit (vol 2)," Dr. M'Clure is described as follows:

> "He was amiable and obliging in his disposition, and always ready to confer a favour when it was in his power... His preaching was characterized by neatness, perspicuity, and accuracy, rather than by great force or point. He was a good scholar; and, though he made no

display of scholarship in his sermons, it was manifest to
all competent judges who heard or read them, that they
were the productions of a well disciplined and well fur-
nished mind."

Rev. Thomas Robbins, November 12, 1852

That highlights who David M'Clure was. Now take a look at where
he stood:

From his sermon on **"The Moral Law – The Existence and Perfections
of God,"**

"He is 'the God not of the Jews only, but also of the Gentiles,' and the
God of universal nature; who made the heavens and the earth, and all
their hosts; eternal, self-existing, uncreated, underived; infinite in all
perfection, most powerful, wise and good; most holy, immutable, just
and true, omniscient, everywhere present, and infinitely happy; the
alone almighty preserver and governor of all things; whose providence
is intimately conversant in all events, directing, permitting and over-
ruling all things for His own glory and the happiness of the universe."

"He is the alone creator and upholder of all things, and on His absolute goodness we are totally dependant for all the good and happiness which we need or hope for throughout the endless periods of
our existance."

"IT is observable that almost all the duties which mankind owe to God
and to one another, are in the decalogue forcibly expressed by negative
precepts. They forbid every species and every degree of evil of <u>thought
and behaviour</u>. And when one virtue or duty is commanded all the
virtues and duties of the same kind are included; and when one vice

or sin is forbidden, all vices and sins of the same species are included in the prohibition, and the opposite virtues commanded."

On **Jesus Christ our Hope**,

"Death and the curse came by the first Adam's eating of the fruit of the interdicted tree; and life and immortality are given to believers, since Christ the second Adam bore death and the curse, on the tree of the cross."

"May we persevere in <u>faith</u> and <u>love</u> and <u>holy obedience</u>, and thro' grace obtain admittance into the everlasting kingdom of our Lord and Saviour Jesus Christ; to whom be all the glory of our salvation."

On Us, from a **1799 New Year's sermon** we call "**The Improve Life**" sermon,

> "NOTHING is more certain than that man is born to die; yet there is no one important truth, less practically believed!"

> "All men think all men mortal but themselves."

> "There are a happy few who make the brevity of life, and a preparation for death, the interesting subjects of their daily <u>devout meditation; and earnestly seek for grace, that they may be prepared</u> for a speedy summons from life, and appear with acceptance before God"

> "Multiplied and various are the calls which God gives to mankind, by his word and providences, to improve life, in preparation for death and eternal scenes."

"This is the first and great commandment: "Thou shalt love the Lord thy God, with <u>all thy heart</u>, and with <u>all thy might</u>, and with <u>all thy mind</u>."

"Most powerful are the motives, which urge and impel us to improve life, in a preparation for that never ending existence"

David M'Clure came to understand God the Father, Christ the Son, The Holy Spirit and our relationship to "The Godhead" in a way that we all should. Through his sermons and teaching, he shared this understanding with us, and we can only benefit from its adoption. I will let M'Clure summarize this understanding,

"The best preparation for Heaven, is 'a conformity to God in holiness'—Let us strive to be holy, that our minds may be Heavenly. And may we be prepared for our departure, should it be THIS YEAR, or this day…"

Robert Boyle (1627 – 1692) Boyle was born Jan. 25, 1627. He is known as the father of Modern Chemistry, the experimental method, peer-reviewed publication, the foundational understanding of "base elements" and "Boyle's Law". He was also one of the great, yet unnoticed theologians. At a time when questioning either established science or endorsed religion was very dangerous, Boyle helped start and operate the "invisible college." When power changed hands in 1660, the invisible college was made official by the king as **The Royal Society**. Boyle was then elected President of the Society but turned it down because it would require him to sign an oath to an entity other than God. Boyle possessed a deep knowledge of Scripture, including its original languages of Hebrew, Greek, Aramaic, and Chaldean in addition to Latin, Syriac, French, and Italian. He personally funded the translation and distribution of the Bible into other languages and even provided for the continuance of his mission work in his will. Firsthand accounts show Boyle "never gave less than £1000 a year" to spreading the Word of God. (*Treatises on the High Veneration Man's Intellect Owes to God*) This is the modern-day equivalent of over $3,000,000 a year! In 1661, Boyle petitioned the King to grant a Royal Charter to a company to bring the Bible to America in a version translated into Algonquin. Boyle was the first "Governor" of "**The New England Company**," an office he held from 1661-1689. The New England Company managed investments in both land and money and then used the whole of its income to support its mission. Still in existence today, The New England Company is Britain's oldest operating missionary society.

Boyle believed the study of science was another means to achieve a greater understanding of God. Boyle wrote, "…the World is the great Book, not so much of Nature, as of the God of Nature, which we should find crowded with instructive Lessons, if we had but the Skill, and would take the Pains, to extract and pick them out." As a scholar of both language and science, Boyle was perhaps the most qualified to comment on any conflict between science and the Bible. His explanation for such an occurrence? Either a mistake in the science or an incorrect interpretation of Scripture. In other words, he believed there was no conflict between science and Scripture, only man's failure in either. To explain the latter, "I am confirmed in the belief, that by transferring our impressions to the Sacred Text, we often impute to the Scriptures our own faults and deficiencies."

Boyle made the case that if "idle hands" were the devil's workshop, then how much more would an idle mind be? His book, *Occasional Reflections*, written in 1665, was dedicated to the practice of maintaining an active mind of intentional thought through observation and reflection. In this book he writes this of the idle mind and the opportunity it provides Satan, "…scarce anything is more in his (father of lies) interest than solicitously to divert men from thinking, and discourage them in it, there being few things whereby he could more effectually oppose at once, both the Glory of God and the good of men…" In an earlier book, *Some considerations touching the style of the Holy Scriptures* written in 1661, Boyle points out the solution: "Sin came into the world by the weakness of one man, listening to the words of the devil; so Divine Wisdom is pleased to make restoring Grace operate on us, in submitting our better understanding to the Word of God."

Boyle believed that, in Scripture and science, we should leave our opinions behind and take from either the truth they offer. Of Scripture he said, "We should obtain our opinions from Scripture rather than take them to Scripture since Scripture is the best expositor of itself."

The same is evidenced in his experimental philosophy for science and could be said, We should obtain our opinions from science rather than take them to science since science is the best expositor of itself. As Boyle put it, there are truths science would never know existed except the Bible tells us so. Boyle: "There are divers truths in the Christian religion, that reason left to itself would never have been able to find out. … Such as … free will … that the world was made in six days, that Christ should be born of a virgin, and that in his person there should be united two such infinitely distant natures as the divine and human; and that the bodies of good men shall be raised from death and so advantageously changed, that the glorified persons shall be like or equal to, the angels." At the age of 14, Boyle took himself to Italy to study Galileo's mathematical theories of science. From this knowledge, he decided science should not be merely passed on but tested. From this came "The Experimental Method" and "Peer-Reviewed Publishing."

Boyle often addressed those who would separate the Old and New Testaments as separate works, viewing the Old as obsolete. One of the best examples of this gave me such an enlightened perspective that I want to share it with you. Boyle said when he read and contemplated the Scriptures he saw them like this, "I sometimes contemplate Moses and Elias (Elijah) talking with Christ — I mean the law and the prophets harmonizing with the Gospel."

I think Bishop Burnet, who spoke at Boyle's funeral in 1692 summed up Boyle's outlook on science and God the best. He said Robert Boyle was "…one of those individuals who have directed all their enquiries into nature to the Honour of its great Maker."

Vance Havner (1901 – 1986) Born in the rural mountains of North Carolina at a place nicknamed "Jugtown," Havner said he didn't know a day when he didn't feel destined to preach. Not unlike the other great people of God we reference, he showed a thirst from a very young age that was accompanied by a drive and mental capacity to embrace the full promise of God and "thirst no more." Nine-year-old Havner taught Sunday school and submitted his first written sermon to the local newspaper for publication. If you ever heard Havner preach, then you have likely heard him tell the story how at the age of twelve he made his petition to be ordained to preach. He tells of going to the church to preach the first time and having to stand on a chair to deliver his sermon, his father on one side and the pastor on the other. Havner achieved his goal of becoming ordained at the age of fifteen. While the "boy-preacher of Jugtown" drew crowds as large as 1800 people, it is what the man-preacher devoted his life to that had an immeasurable impact on "The Church" and the churches claiming Christ's name.

After several attempts to pursue the traditional track of college and church pastorship, Havner found himself distracted by the influences of "Liberalism" and "Modernism." He said that this was a time during which he moved away from adherence to Scripture. This path, however, left him unsuccessful in his preaching and unsatisfied in his faith. It was at this moment of discontent that God placed in his hands a book titled *Christianity and Liberalism* by J. Gresham Machen. This study into the differences between Biblical Christianity and the theology of Modernism both firmly secured his foundation in fundamentalist faith and set his feet on the path of confronting the plague that had tempted him. Afterward, he said, "The word of God is either absolute or obsolete."

Havner's ministry seemed to be summed up in this one quote, "It's hard to be optimistic, with misty optics." Havner set out to be a missionary to his own people leading and pleading for Revival everywhere he went, saying, "I have come to comfort the afflicted and to afflict the comfortable." But Havner was not a party planner. He preached "Real Revival" is simply living "New Testament Christianity, the saints going back to normal." "Real revival does not begin with joyous singing. It begins with conviction and repentance on the part of Christians." Like others who put their service to God above public opinion, no one's toes were safe, not even the pastor, "The preacher who is concerned with gaining a reputation, rising in his profession, is always in bondage. The itch for bigness is a dangerous thing. It has made a castaway of many a man whom God once richly blessed." It was not unheard of to hear Havner quote Tozer and vice versa, as both stood strongly for the "Lordship" of Christ as reflected in this Havner quote, "No man can be a Christian by knowingly and willfully taking on Christ on the installment plan, as Savior now, and Lord later."

During his ministry, Havner was in huge demand, teaching a return to the Gospel in over 13,000 sermons in churches, colleges, and any meeting that opened their doors. His recorded sermons still play on some radio stations to this day. You can listen to his words easily with access to the Internet. Havner also sought to clean those "optics" through the written word. Approaching 40 books and seemingly endless published articles, his message rings as true today as ever.

Billy Graham said of his preaching that "...he used the Bible like a sword." "He could preach the most powerful sermons with conviction, and the conviction could settle upon the audience and they would hang on every word." Havner's brother-in-law, Joe Allred, said this of

Havner, "Seven days a week, 24 hours a day, he was a Christian man." What more could we want to be remembered of us while we are living and when we have gone than this? Havner spread the word of God for 72 years in life and continues decades after death. Vance Havner left us a simple warning we can use to set the standard of a 24/7 Christian: "God judges what we tolerate as well as what we practice. Too often we put up with things we ought to put out."

Matthew Henry (1662-1714) Writing Henry's bio was laborious but interesting and instructive. As we wander through his life we will find a consistency to which all who claim to believe and serve should aspire. His house was a "house of God" whether it was his family home or the house of worship he shepherded. With that, here is Matthew Henry.

An important factor in Matthew Henry's life actually occurred before his birth. "The Act of Uniformity" had come into effect on August 24, 1662, affecting nearly two thousand pastors including Henry's father who said it interfered with "Training up a child in the way he should go." Those who would not sign in agreement to this bureaucratic overreach could neither teach at nor graduate from either Oxford or Cambridge and were branded "Dessenters." As a result, Henry's upbringing was carried out under what Rev. Doolittle would call, "the persecuting temper of the times," or the government's pressure to conform to their religious mandate.

Born on the 18th of October, 1662, at Broad Oak, Henry was able to read a chapter in the Bible very clearly and with some understanding at about three-years-old. A relative and childhood friend of Henry's said childish years were over in him sooner than in other persons; he very early put away childish things. Henry said that it was at the age of ten, after hearing one of his father's sermons on the 51rst Psalm, that he felt the conviction of sin. It was in this same year that young Henry had a relentless fever that left everyone believing he would die at any time. Helping them through this time was the widow of the Rev. Zachary Thomas. On returning from a ministry trip Philip Henry told his family and Mrs. Thomas, "At such a place and time upon the road, I did most solemnly, freely, and deliberately resign up my dear child unto God, to do what he pleased with him and me." Mrs. Thomas replied, "And I believe, sir, in that place and time God gave him back to you again." It is also recorded that after this he quickly recovered. His sister, who gave this account, had this to say of the event, "Though I was then but a child of eight years old, and could think but as a child, I was very much affected with that discourse between my father and Mrs. Thomas; it tended to endear my brother the more to me, since I really believed he was given to us back again in an extraordinary manner."

In his writings, he records his conversion the following year at the age of eleven. He committed that "...his faith and comfort might not stand in the wisdom of men, but the word of God." This began a practice of the search, study, and understanding of the Scriptures as the foundation of all he said and did. Henry quickly gained a reputation for learning very quickly and retaining what he learned. The combination of these talents gave him an advantage in his efforts to acquire knowledge. In fact, at times, his mother would become concerned that he would overdo it and resolved herself to call the young Henry from his closet of self-confinement and study and send him outside to take a walk in the fields to protect his health.

From his beginnings reading the Holy Scriptures at age three through his formative years, Henry was drawn to God's message. He delighted not only in reading the Bible but in understanding the very sense of its meaning. A teenage Henry so enjoyed the ministers with whom he became acquainted he would often write down the sermons he heard from them and then respectfully and earnestly repeat them. This was just one of the advantages of growing up the son of Philip Henry. Through his father's tutelage, the son Henry became an expert of Hebrew and the other "learned languages." In 1680, Philip sent his son to live with the Rev. Thomas Doolittle in Islington, London to further his education. Upon his return in 1682 at the age of twenty, Henry penned a list of "Mercies Received" from God and signed it. Here are a couple of excerpts which give some insights into the mind of Matthew Henry:

> "That I have been born in a place and time of gospel light; that I have had the Scriptures, and means for understanding them, by daily expositions and many good books; and that I have had a heart to give myself to and delight in the study of them."

> "That I have had some sight of the majesty of God, the sweetness of Christ, the evil of sin, the worth of my soul, the vanity of the world, and the reality and weight of invisible things…That when I have been in doubt, I have been guided; in danger, I have been guarded; in temptation, I have been succored (assisted, relieved); under guilt, I have been pardoned; when I have prayed, I have been heard and answered; when I have been under afflictions, they have been sanctified, and all by Divine grace."

In 1685, Philip Henry again sent his son Matthew to London, Gray's Inn, so that he could study the law. It was not Philip's intention that his son would make it his profession, but that through it he would improve in usefulness. He did. Here too he excelled searching and learning both the human laws and the Divine. At Gray's Inn at age twenty-three, Henry not only promoted the practice of social prayer and religious discussion among his friends, often he would share his understanding, his aforementioned sense, of the Scriptures with them.

Around the year 1686, Henry found himself in Chester, his reputation having caused the people there to invite him to teach them. After only a few days, and after impressing some of the greatest "dissenters" in Chester with his address, he was given the invitation to become their preacher. In London on May 9th, 1687, Matthew Henry was ordained the Reverend Matthew Henry and would return to Chester to minister there for many years.

Before beginning this ministry, Henry engaged in a practice that he started when he was young and would continue until his death – "self-scrutiny." This is what he recorded:

"It is a common saying, that the end specifies the action; and, therefore, it is of great consequence to fix that right, that the eye may be single, for otherwise it is an evil eye. A bye and base end will certainly spoil the acceptableness of the best actions that can be performed. Now, what is the mark I aim at in this great turn of my life? Let conscience be faithful herein, and let the Searcher of hearts make me known to myself."

1. "I think I can say, with confidence, that I do not design to take up the ministry as a trade to live by, or to enrich myself by, out of the greediness of filthy lucre. No! I hope I aim at nothing but souls; and if I gain those, though I should lose all my worldly comforts by it, I shall reckon myself to have made a good bargain.

2. I think I can say, with as much assurance, that my design is not to get myself a name amongst men, or to be talked of in the world, as one that makes somewhat of a figure. No; that is a poor business. If I have but a good name with God, I think I have enough, though among men I be reviled, and

have my name trampled upon as mire in the streets. I prefer the good word of my Master far before the good word of my fellow-servants.

3. I can appeal to God, that I have no design in the least to maintain a party, or to keep up any schismatical faction; my heart rises against the thoughts of it. I hate dividing principles and practices, and what ever others are, I am for peace and healing; and if my blood would be sufficient balsam, I would gladly part with the last drop of it, for the closing up of the bleeding wounds of differences that are amongst true christians. Peace is such a precious jewel, that I would give anything for it but truth. Those who are hot and bitter in their contendings for or against little things, and zealous in keeping up names of division and maintaining parties, are of a spirit which I understand not. Let not my soul come into their secret."

"My ends then are according to my principles, and I humbly appeal to God concerning the integrity of my heart in them."

"That I deliberately place the glory of God as my highest and ultimate end, and if I can be but any ways instrumental to promote that, I shall gain my end and have my desire. I do not design to preach myself, but as a faithful friend of the Bridegroom, to preach Christ Jesus my Lord, as the standard-bearer among ten thousands."

Henry's life, however, should be an example to us all, that a commitment such as this does not mean a life free of attacks from Satan or the need to live above them. Of this, we have a detailed record, as Henry, now "head of a house" began and continued to keep a diary. After beginning his ministry in Chester, Henry met and married Katherine, who eighteen months later gave birth to a daughter giving her life in the process as a result of small-pox. Henry would name this daughter Katherine. Henry would later take a new bride, Mary. He would ultimately have one son named for his father, Philip, and eight daughters, three of which he would watch die in infancy. Henry would go on to see the death of both his parents, two sisters and two brothers-in-law. With the loss of his sisters, Henry would take in or make arrangements for the care and love of their children.

Henry would raise and guard his children and his house the same as he would raise and guard his flock, God's house. In the morning, as in Sunday service, there would be prayer and praise and the reading of a few verses from the Old Testament. In the evening, as in evening service, there would again be prayer and praise and reading a few verses from the New Testament. It was said that when he taught the meaning of the Scriptures read "He gave the sense, even where it was the most intricate, in a plain and familiar expression, which not only made it intelligible, but pleasant and satisfactory to the mind that received it." And when he prayed it was "with an almost inimitable liveliness of affection, and tenderness of spirit, with great propriety of petitions to the case of the family, and of every one in it, and of his friends that were so happy as to be present with him at that duty."

Henry's diary also showed his solemn commitment represented years earlier. Henry observed the anniversary of any remarkable providence, relating to himself and his family: if the event brought affliction it was remembered as a time of humility; if an act of mercy, it was remembered with praise; and regardless, it was a time of sincere prayer that "the sanctifying fruits might still remain and increase" (that their effect for the kingdom would continue).

Henry's diary also recorded annual reflections on both his birthday and the new year. In 1701, "having finished the thirty-ninth year of (his) pilgrimage," he writes; "I continue hitherto, knowing whom I have trusted, and trusting Him whom I have known. The greatest comfort of my life has been, that God has been pleased to use me for his service; and my greatest grief, that I have been so little serviceable to him."

On New Year's every year he would renew his commitment, his "bond," with God: "May I ever be free in thy service, and never desire to be free from it. Nail my ear to thy door-post, and let me serve thee for ever."

When a member of his flock wandered, he would not ignore, tolerate, or justify it. He would follow the instructions in the Manual to go to them directly and would, without bias, ask them whether it was true. If it was, he addressed the sin unequivocally, stating it for what it was, evil. Then, in the name of God, he would call on them to repent, and, when they did, he rejoiced. On the occasion that they did not, Henry's heart broke for them as reflected in this entry: "I have labored with _____, to set before him the evil of his sin; O that I could see him duly affected; but nothing less than the grace of God will do it."

Henry was also joyed to continue his father's (Philip) work. He loved to promote and preach for the cause of Reformation. He held a circle of thirty miles where he would take time during his week to travel and support other churches and ministers in this cause. Above his duties as a minister, Henry managed the immense feat of many publications; he published a variety of treatises, sermons, catechisms, hymns and more. Among them are his works on Meekness, Communion with God, The

Pleasantness of a Religious Life and Prayer, etc. All were well known and well studied by many. But that was not enough. He also produced the still well-known and referenced *Exposition of the Old and New Testament*. Yes, he not only read it and studied it, but he also wrote and published his "sense" of every word of it! Sadly, while his notes were complete of the entire book, he had only produced to final publication Genesis through Acts. However, his works were so well known and so well respected that immediately upon his death many called for the publication of the rest. Several eminent ministers of the time were chosen for this honor. And honor him they did as they sought to respect his heart, expressed in Volume 1 of this great work: "This night, after many thoughts of heart, and many prayers concerning it, I began my notes on the Old Testament. It is not likely I should live to finish it, or if I should, that it should be of public service, for I am not par negotio, (equal to the work) yet, in the strength of God, and I hope with a single eye to his glory, I set about it;… I go about it with fear and trembling, lest I exercise myself in things too high for me,"

Living only fifty-two years, Henry accomplished and contributed more than most who live decades more. He didn't do it for fame or title but out of a personal, cordial commitment to God made as a young boy and intentionally kept throughout a lifetime. As a "Dessenter," Henry would spend his lifetime teaching religious liberty and freedom from government and a complete necessity for commitment to God, which is reflected in this quote: "It is better to be serving God in solitude than serving sin in a multitude."

Finally, from Rev. W. Tong, who gave one of many memorial services upon Matthew Henry's passing on July 11th, 1714:

"In him you had the happy mixture of great strength of judgment and fervour of spirit. Some are very zealous, but not so judicious; others judicious but not so zealous: he was both a burning and a shining light. In him you had a true greatness of soul, mixed with exemplary modesty and humility…In his preaching you had a very just and close way of thinking, with the most plain, proper, natural and easy expression, and a great regard to the honour of Christ and free grace, joined with a constant endeavour to beat down sin, and revive the power and practice of godliness" Henry was, "one that was wonderfully fitted to feed the lambs of the flock."

The Lady Julian (~1342 – unknown) Very little is known about her other than what can be gathered from her own written record. Even that, however, is intentionally limited, as Lady Julian took the position that others should be more concerned with paying attention to what God had to say than the person charged with delivering it. She said, "I beg you all for God's sake and advise you all for your own advantage that you stop paying attention to the poor, worldly, sinful creature to whom this vision was shown, and eagerly, attentively, lovingly and humbly contemplate God, who in His gracious love and in His eternal goodness wanted the vision to be generally known to comfort us all." In fact, in her second writing, she removed details about herself.

Lady Julian's given name is unknown. The name "Julian" came from the church of St. Julian where she lived in a room attached to the church. You see, Lady Julian was what was known as an "anchoress." In her time, such roles were not completely uncommon and had been adopted by those seeking a deeper personal understanding of and relationship to God. While we might mistake an anchoress as a kind of nun, the anchoress might more accurately be compared to a reclusive monk, not because of their religious beliefs but because of their approach in practicing them. Lady Julian's life was typical of such a commitment to the pursuit of God. As stated, she lived in a room attached to the church. This room had a window that opened into the sanctuary so that she could observe any service. Anchorites (men) and anchoresses (women) were expected to share the fruits of their solitary study with others, and Lady Julian was no exception. These devout followers of God provided council and spiritual support to the "flock." It is not clear when she died, only that she was still alive in 1413.

Acknowledging the stated history, The Lady Julian was no average anchoress; The Lady Julian was no average Christian. Lady Julian prayed that God would make her experience the pain and suffering of "The Passion" that she might better understand what Christ went through in paying the price for her sin. She wanted to understand, physically, mentally, and spiritually the suffering He experienced on her behalf. She prayed to be made sick, to be brought to the brink of death, and "to have more (understanding) by the Grace of God." While it is unclear exactly when she made the request, she records that, "This sickness desired I in my thought that I might have it when I were thirty years old." Later, she records "when I was thirty winters old and a half, God sent me a bodily sickness." Within days, the Parson was called in. Her hands fell to her sides, her head tipped into her pillow, her mother reached up to close her eyes and all thought she was dead. After she had received her "revelations" she quickly recovered and documented what had been revealed. What is known of her experience and that to which we refer comes from the first manuscript, *Comfortable Words for Christ's Lovers*, which she recorded following her experience on May 8, 1373. Most people, however, reference the later version, *Revelations of Divine Love*, which was written down some twenty years later, after experience and reflection gave her a greater understanding of the event previously recorded.

Lady Julian wrote that she was "oned to God" and that by an "inner Light (spiritual sight)" He provided her with revelations of His Divine Truth. She also says that things were revealed "By bodily Sight" and states plainly that "I have said as I saw, as truly as I can." Finally, Lady Julian declares Truths to be revealed "By words formed in mine understanding (mind)" of which she says "as for the words formed, I have said them right as our Lord showed me them." Although she defined her communion with God taking three different forms, she references them as one indivisible experience, "these three be so oned, as to my understanding, that I cannot nor may disport (separate) them."

So, why take note of an obscure writing from a reclusive woman who lived in the 14th century? The experience she describes in her writing was the result of a prayer and sincere desire few today would have the courage and commitment to ask for. Lady Julian wanted to know the Passion of Christ, not just so that she might understand and be closer to Christ, but that others might as well. She ends with a prayer and closing guidance:

> "I pray to the Almighty God that this book come only into the hands of those who want to love Him faithfully... for this revelation is deep theology and great wisdom, so it must not remain with anyone who is thrall (a slave) to sin and the Devil." And "Beware that you do not take one thing according to your taste and fancy and leave another, for that is what heretics do."

Sir John Baggot Glubb (1897 – 1986) Born in 1897 as the son of an officer in the Royal Engineers, his childhood would be one of travel and exposure to a bigger world. By the age of ten, Sir John had already called more than one place home and had been sent to school in Switzerland for a year. At the age of seventeen, he entered the Royal Military Academy at Woolrich and, like his father, was commissioned in the Royal Engineers less than a year later. Stationed in Belgium and France during the First World War, he had been wounded three times and received the Military Cross. At the age of twenty-three, he volunteered for service in Iraq. Sir John said, "I originally went to Iraq in 1920…seeking fresh fields of adventure and a wider knowledge of the many different forms of soldiering." Six years later, he resigned his commission in the British Army to accept an administrative position within the Iraqi Government. Sir John took this position with this stand, "I strenuously opposed any idea that East was East and West was West and that the two could never agree. I had experienced in myself, as I thought, the feasibility of living simultaneously as an Arab amongst Arabs and an Englishman amongst Europeans. Why should not the two work hand in hand?" In 1930, a now thirty-three-year-old Sir John signed a contract with what is now Jordan. The next year he formed the "Desert Patrol" to confront a raiding problem in the south of the country. Eight years later, he was appointed to command the Jordan Arab Legion (Jordan Army). Sir John made the J.A.L. an elite force that would become famous throughout the world. During the 1948 Arab-Israeli War, Sir John led the J.A.L. across the River Jordan into the West Bank and maintained its defense after the armistice in 1949. Throughout his career, Sir John was awarded 17 other Honors in addition to the Military Cross. After the murder of King Abdulla in 1951, the "genuine feeling of friendship" gave way to "the flood of hate." On February 29, 1956, after 26 years of service, he was ordered to leave the country within two hours. Sir John, by his own admission, "… had failed hopelessly in the task to which I had devoted nearly all my life – to promote ever closer co-operation and understanding between the East and the West."

In addition to two sons (one dying after only a few weeks), Sir John and his wife adopted a Bedouin girl and two Palestinian children. After leaving Jordan in 1956, Sir John lectured across the United States, Britain, and greater Europe. In this time, he also published seventeen books on the Middle East. King Hussein of Jordan, his former friend, spoke at his funeral in 1986. His writings have been preserved in the Middle East Archive at St Anthony's College in Oxford.

He ended his book, *A Soldier With The Arabs*, with these lines: "God rarely creates an old head on young shoulders. Most of us have to gain our experience the hard way." "Finally, let us remember that from the soil of what is now Jordan sprang up the three greatest religions of mankind, Judaism, Islam and Christianity. This little tract of land has done more to bring the human race closer to God, than have all the vast continents by which it is surrounded."

St. Bernard of Clairvaux (1090-1153) Bernard was born at Fontaines near Dijon, France to Tescelin, lord of Fontaines and Aleth of Montbard. He was one of seven children. At the age of nine, about the time his mother died, he was sent to school at Chatillon-sur-Seine. It is recorded that he had a love for poetry and literature in general, preparing him for the study of the Sacred Texts. In the year 1111, at the age of 20, Bernard left his home to join the monastic community of Citeaux. His five brothers, two uncles, and some 30 young noblemen followed him. It wasn't long before St. Stephen sent the young Bernard to found a new house at Vallée d'Absinthe, or Valley of Bitterness, in the Diocese of Langres. On June 25th, 1115, Bernard named the new house Claire Vallée, or Clairvaux, the Valley of Light. From that day forward, Bernard and Clairvaux would forever be entwined. Bernard demanded a lot of himself as well as others. Early on, a struggle with some health issues taught him the virtues of patience. William of Champeaux, Bishop and professor of theology at Notre Dame, had become Bernard's good friend after giving him the title of abbot. It was the support of this friend that aided him through this tumultuous time.

Bernard's calling was clear. Under his leadership, Clairvaux drew huge numbers, soon outgrowing its capacity. As a result, new houses were founded to accommodate the crowds. In 1118, Three Fountains was founded; in 1119, Fontenay; and in 1121, Foigny. In all, Bernard would seed one hundred and sixty-three new houses in his lifetime. In 1120, Bernard composed his first work, *De Gradibus Superbiae et Humilitatis*, and his homilies entitled *De Laudibus Mariae*. Bernard met with immediate pushback for the "impracticable" standards he set. Bernard met his accusers head-on, both with respect and the patience he had learned years earlier. As a result, not only were his positions accepted but a restoration moved across the church as bishops, clergy, and other faithful who had slid into a "worldly life" converted to his positions and returned to a disciplined pursuit. It was about this time that he penned, *Grace and Free Will.*

In 1128, the bishops made Bernard secretary of the council of Troyes and charged him with drawing up the synodal statutes. The council had been formed to settle disputes, and following the council, the Bishop of Verdun was deposed. As a result, once again, politics raised its serpent-like head to attack him. There came unfounded accusations, which prevailed even in Rome where he was proclaimed a monk who meddled with matters that did not concern him. Cardinal Harmeric, on behalf of the pope, wrote Bernard an official letter of reproof. In it, he said, "It is not fitting that noisy and troublesome frogs should come out of their marshes to trouble the Holy See and the cardinals." As before, Bernard answered the charge directly by pointing out that any assistance he provided the council was not from his desire but because it had been required of him. Bernard then skillfully turns the argument around on his accuser saying: "Now illustrious Harmeric, if you so wished, who would have been more capable of freeing me from the necessity of assisting at the council than yourself? Forbid those noisy troublesome frogs to come out of their holes, to leave their marshes ... Then your friend will no longer be exposed to the accusations of pride and presumption." Impressed by Bernard's response, the cardinal, the Holy See and the church again saw the wisdom in his words and reversed their position. Following these events, Bernard framed the Rule of the Knights Templar.

Fighting against "Heresy" would be Bernard's life. Although he would have been happy and even preferred to have lived out his days studying and ministering at the monastery, he was continuously called out to defend a standard that politicians within the church sought to "let go." Every time, Bernard's wisdom and ability to relate that wisdom would beat back the world that fought to corrupt the church and defame the God he loved. One such occurrence was in 1147/1148 and was brought by Gilbert de la Porée, Bishop of Poitiers, who proposed that "the essence and the attributes of God are not God, that the properties of the Persons of the Trinity are not the persons themselves." Bernard's arguments against these and other claims by Gilbert were embraced by the church and Gilbert's assertions denounced.

Finally, while Bernard is credited with initiating the Crusade to push back attacks and raids on the route from Jeruselum with his Templars, misconduct, political agendas, lack of discipline and treason among Christian nobles took the Crusade off track and resulted in its failure and historical disgrace. To this, Bernard, in the second part of his *Book of Consideration* explains, "…with the crusaders as with the Hebrew people, in whose favour the Lord had multiplied his prodigies, their sins were the cause of their misfortune and miseries."

Bernard died at the age of 63, remembered with the title of "Doctor of the Church" and honored by the Cistercians as "founder." St. Bernard of Clairvaux's life represented a simple principle that he would remind himself of every morning:

"Why have I come here?... To lead a holy life."

About the Author

At this point, the book is written and nearly through its second pass by my editor. Until now, I have resisted doing an "About the Author" narrative. As I mention in the Preface, "This also caused another result I did not plan for or quite honestly want... 'It's time to write a book... or books." Any such book should be a Work of God or should not be at all. My prayer – before, during and after the production of the book – is that not a single word be mine.

So, what are you reading then? In recent weeks, we have been reading the autobiography of W.P. Nicholson, *To God Be The Glory*. Hearing how his life moved toward God and how his ministry for God developed didn't take away from the message he offered. His story didn't change God's message, but it gave his unique delivery context. So, here is not my life's story but a little context.

I am the product of Exposure. Exposure to many Christian denominations and many points of view. Exposure to church growth, church shrinkage and, sadly, church splits. I have seen great vessels of God's message and watched people suffer at the hands of a "Hireling." I have lived amongst the Sincere and the Self-serving. I have been Exposed to the many man-made faces of God and the Glory of the real thing.

As a child, my mother took me to the local Baptist church most Sunday mornings. The church building could literally fit the buildings of the entire town inside. No, the church was not huge; the town consisted of a small grocery store and the smallest post office you could imagine... and then subtract 20%. It was in a tiny, 2nd grade Sunday school room that I first embraced Christ as my Savior. During this time, I attended the church youth group. It was also there that I learned what was written in the Bible, for which I will always be grateful. Along with these Baptist activities, my Grandparents brought me to evening services at the Free Methodist Church where I was also enrolled in their youth program. As my best friend was Catholic, I also had regular visits to Saturday Mass and Catechism, which I was kicked out of for teasing the girls and being a general disruption. (My Mom would have been devastated had she known.)

When in my teens, my father began attending church with us but wanted something different, so we began attending the United Methodist church in an even smaller town. Yes, smaller. A smaller grocery that had closed a few years earlier and an old John Deere dealer that was now basically a tractor mechanic with a wood-burning stove that the local farmers would sit around and talk (men don't "gossip"). My old best friend, the son of an alcoholic, had given into drugs and we parted ways. My new best friend attended the Congregational church in the town where my school was located – a huge metropolis with nearly a dozen businesses. His mom had been killed in a car accident when he was only a couple years old and his father had left, leaving him and his siblings to be raised by their Grandparents. On the occasion that I stayed over Saturday night, we went to church Sunday morning – not optional.

During my teenage years at the United Methodist Church, I taught Sunday School, collected and turned in the offering, and joined the choir. I had also tied for the longest continuing attendance with the wife of the tractor mechanic. First, they gave you a pin, then a wreath, and then bars to hang beneath each year. In my mid-twenties, I asked to stop receiving the bars as I had reached 17 years. Aside from all this, two very important things happened while I attended that church. When I approached the age of twelve, I attended confirmation classes taught by two of my schoolteachers. One we will talk about again. The class is meant to teach you about the church, its doctrines, and the responsibility of church membership. When you finished the class, you were asked if you wanted to become a member of the church… what's a twelve-year-old going to say? Yes, obviously. Well, except for me; I told my mentors that, while they had shown me nothing with which I disagreed, they could not guarantee this would remain true. I said that, while God would remain constant, man would always fall, and I would not sign my allegiance to that man.

Soon after confirmation, one of the teachers and other adults from the church daringly took a band of us to Ichthus in Kentucky (a weekend-long Christian concert). I so enjoyed the experience that, as soon as I could drive, I began bringing others to Ichthus. In my early twenties, I was asked to be the photographer for a media outlet in Canada, which supplied me with a press pass and "access."

Within a couple of years following the confirmation class, a few other students, that same confirmation teacher, and I started a Fellowship of Christian Athletes at our High School. With this advancement of their children in the social scene, my parents opened our home to young people. I also attended the monthly meeting of my father's Christian Businessmen's Association where I ran the sound and produced the recordings of the speakers. It was at one of these meetings, at the age of seventeen, listening to the testimony of a convicted murderer that I re-committed my life to Christ. As I entered into my college years, which included InterVarsity Christian Fellowship, the crowd increased. The annual camp meeting that my family had attended for years had become a gathering place for thirty to forty youth. My brother had combined his circle with my sister's, and most of the "group" began to attend our little church.

It was during this period that I met both a great "vessel of God's message" and a "hireling." The first embraced the youth and their independent fervor for Christ. By so doing, our little church that previously averaged an attendance of five to twenty on any given Sunday topped One Hundred and Twenty-Five with standing room only. Sadly, this man of God retired, appropriately, in the town of Paradise, Michigan. He was replaced with a well-packaged hireling, a wolf in sheep's clothing, you might say. This man, crippled with Cerebral Palsy and blind, was a sympathetic figure. But this man wanted the glory for himself. He demanded the youth become members of the church or forgo activities there. He singled out the weak "sheep" in the group sowing the seeds of discontent. This man sought to show the parent church that he was driving a boom and would need to leave the little stone church behind and build a big new church. He even had the property picked out and had "claimed" it in the name of Christ.

In defending the standard set by the former pastor and the movement of the Spirit who flowed from this group of young people, my family and I found ourselves at the center of a church battle. Something that could not have even been imagined by the church "family" only months earlier. People I had known and been raised amongst my entire life would side against us saying unthinkable things. People who had babysat me as a young child. People who, when I had finished introducing my new date to my parents, had us drive to their house as well for approval. I did not understand. I did recognize, however, that what I had told my confirmation teacher more than a dozen years earlier had come true; the men and women of that church had taken ungodly positions, and I wanted no part of it. Having seen too many church splits, we did not endorse such action; we simply left, quieting any noise some allies wanted to make. In the years following, most of those "family" members who attacked us apologized. They had seen firsthand the difference between a move of God and the aspirations of man. The little stone church is still their home today with an attendance that averages from five to twenty on any given Sunday.

An interesting thought occurred to me while writing this part. No, the hireling never got his church claimed in Christ's name, but Christ did. Today, a church of another denomination stands there. The man who had been my confirmation teacher and mentor quit his job as a public-school teacher and became a Minister for the United Methodist Church. Later, he left, and now pastors a non-denominational church. When I saw him recently, he said that, had I done as well in school as I did with my "Final Message from Ma" that I gave at her funeral (part of which is included in chapter 1), I would have gotten better grades. Showing again, as he always had, being a Man of God does not mean you have to be a man without humor.

Since that time at the little stone church, I have visited many denominations including Assemblies of God, Nazarene, and non-denominational. I have participated in God's work wherever He has placed me but still have never "joined" any of man's. It is only in recent years that I looked back and saw this path for what it was. I had never before realized that that twelve-year-old boy had been given the knowledge that was the seed of wisdom yet unrealized. I have been Exposed to "Life" and "Death" in the church and have chosen to die to man's world that I might Rise with Christ to Live in God's. Today, from the perspective of a life always present but never joining, I can step out and look at what man has done. From this place and God's guidance, I can Distinguish Truth and Relay His **Offer of Hope** to others.

Resources

Tozer Resources

Tozer, A.W. "Tozer Audio Sermons." *The Alliance*, www.cmalliance. org/resources/tozer-audio-sermons/

Tozer, A. W. *The Pursuit of God: the Human Thirst for the Divine.* Christian Publications, Inc., 1997.

Tozer, A. W., and Lyle W. Dorsett. *Tozer Speaks to Students: Chapel Messages Preached at Wheaton College.* WingSpread Publishers, 2010.

Tozer, A. W. *The Root of the Righteous: Tapping the Bedrock of True Spirituality.* Christian Publications, 1986.

Tozer, A. W., and Harry Verploegh. *The Set of the Sail.* WingSpread Publishers, 2009.

Havner Resources

Havner, Vance. "Vance Havner (1901 - 1986)." *SermonIndex Audio Sermons*, www.sermonindex.net/modules/mydownloads/viewcat. php?op=&cid=25

Boyle Resources

Boyle, Robert. "Some Considerations Touching the Style of the Holy Scriptures. Rendered into Modern Language, by P. Panter." *Google Play*, Google, 1661, http://play.google.com/books/reader?id=HN

sGAAAAQAAJ&printsec=frontcover&output=reader&hl=en&p
g=GBS.PR6

Boyle, Robert, Michael Hunter, Edward B. Davis. *The Works of Robert Boyle. Unpublished Writings, "On the Diversity of Religions" c. 1670-91, Lists of Boyle's Unpublished Writings, 1650-1744, Index.* Vol. 14, pp. 255-6 and 237. Pickering & Chatto, 2016.

Boyle, Robert. "The Christian Virtuoso; Shewing, That by Being Addicted to Experimental Philosophy, a Man Is Rather Assisted, than Indisposed, to Be a Good Christian : Boyle, Robert, 1627-1691 : Free Download, Borrow, and Streaming." *Internet Archive*, In the Savoy [London] Printed by E. Jones, for J. Taylor, 1690, https://archive.org/details/christianvirtu00boyluoft/page/n7/mode/2up

Boyle, Robert, and Henry Rogers. *Treatises on the High Veneration Man's Intellect Owes to God: on Things above Reason: and on the Style of the Holy Scriptures.* Printed and Published by J. Rickerby, 1836.

Boyle, Robert. "Occasional Reflections upon Several Subjects. With a Discourse about Such Kind of Thoughts : Boyle, Robert, 1665: Free Download, Borrow, and Streaming." *Internet Archive*, 1 Jan. 1970, Oxford, A. A. Masson, 1848. https://archive.org/details/occasionalreflec00boyl/page/n6/mode/2up

Matthew Henry

Henry, Matthew. *Genesis 1 Matthew Henry's Commentary on the Whole Bible*, https://biblehub.com/commentaries/mhcw/genesis/1.htm

Thomas, B. "Matthew Henry." *Conservapedia*, 2020, https://www.conservapedia.com/Matthew_Henry

Alexander, J. W. "Christian Biography: Lives of William Cowper, Mrs. Ann H. Judson, Anna Jane Linnard, Matthew Henry." *Google Play*, Google, https://play.google.com/books/reader?id=tKoXAAAAYA AJ&hl=en&pg=GBS.RA3-PA3

Tong, W., and John Reynolds. "The Miscellaneous Works of the Rev. Matthew Henry, Containing in Addition to Those Heretofore Published, Numerous Sermons Now First Printed from the Original Mss. : an Appendix on What Christ Is Made to Believers,in Forty Real Benefits,by Philip Henry... : Funeral Sermons for Mr. and Mrs. Henry, by the Rev. Matthew Henry : Funeral Sermons on Mr. Matthew Henry, by W. Tong, John Reynolds, and Dr. Williams." *Google Play*, Google, https://play.google.com/books/reader?id=1 mYKssdLzekC&hl=en&pg=GBS.PA733

St. Bernard of Clairvaux

Clairvaux, Bernard. "On Loving God." *Christian Classics Ethereal Library*, https://ccel.org/ccel/bernard/loving_god.html

Clairvaux, Bernard. "On Loving God St Bernard Of Clairvaux : Free Download, Borrow, and Streaming." *Internet Archive*, https:// archive.org/details/OnLovingGodStBernardOfClairvaux/ mode/2up

Lady Julian

Julian, Lady. "Comfortable Words for Christ's Lovers : Being the Visions and Voices Vouchsafed to Lady Julian, Recluse at Norwich in 1373 : Julian, of Norwich, b. 1343 : Free Download, Borrow, and

Streaming." *Internet Archive*, London : H.R. Allenson, 1373, https://archive.org/details/comfortablewords00juliiala/mode/2up

Sir John Baggot Glubb

Glubb, John Baggot. "TheFateofEmpiresbySirJohnGlubb.pdf (PDFy Mirror) : Free Download, Borrow, and Streaming." *Internet Archive*, William Blackwood & Sons Ltd , 1 Jan. 2014, https://archive.org/details/pdfy-2F_iHS6BLtGJb2ad

David M'Clure

M'Clure, David. "Improve Life Sermon 1799." *Pursuit of Character*, 13 Mar. 2016, http://pursuitofcharacter.org/improve-life-sermon-1799/

M'Clure, David. "Sermons on The Moral Law, Justified by Christ." *Pursuit of Character*, 25 Jan. 2019, http://pursuitofcharacter.org/justified-by-christ/

Other Resources

"St. Bernard of Clairvaux." *CATHOLIC ENCYCLOPEDIA: St. Bernard of Clairvaux*, www.newadvent.org/cathen/02498d.htm

"SIMON WHO THE SORY BEHIND A PLAYGROUND FAVORITE." *SIMON WHO THE SORY BEHIND A PLAYGROUND FAVORITE*, July 2011, https://content-usa-today.blogspot.com/2011/07/simon-who-sory-behind-playground.html

Renner, Rick. "Who Were the Nicolaitans, And What Was Their Doctrine and Deeds?" *Rick Renner Ministries*, 27 Aug. 2016, https://renner.org/who-were-nicolaitans-what-was-doctrine-deeds/

"Who Are the Nicolaitans? Bible Meaning and Definition." *Bible Study Tools*, www.biblestudytools.com/dictionary/nicolaitans/

Leisola, Matti, and Jonathan Witt. *Heretic: One Scientist's Journey from Darwin to Design*. Discovery Institute Press, 2018.

McLanahan, Sara, and Gary Sandeful. *Growing up with a Single Parent: What Hurts, What Helps*. Harvard University Press, 1996.

Wilcox, W. Bradford, et al. "*The Evolution of Divorce.*" *National Affairs*, 2009, https://nationalaffairs.com/publications/detail/the-evolution-of-divorce

McLanahan, Sara, et al. *The Future of Children: Fall 2005*. Woodrow Wilson School of Public and International Affairs, Princeton University, 2005.

"Suicide Rates Rising across the U.S." *Centers for Disease Control and Prevention*, Centers for Disease Control and Prevention, 7 June 2018, www.cdc.gov/media/releases/2018/p0607-suicide-prevention.html

"Suicide Rising across the US." *Centers for Disease Control and Prevention*, Centers for Disease Control and Prevention, 7 June 2018, www.cdc.gov/vitalsigns/suicide/

O'Donnell, Jayne, and Anne Saker. "Teen Suicide Is Soaring. Do Spotty Mental Health and Addiction Treatment Share Blame?" *USA Today*, Gannett Satellite Information Network, 20 Mar. 2018, www.usatoday.com/story/news/politics/2018/03/19/teen-suicide-soaring-do-spotty-mental-health-and-addiction-treatment-share-blame/428148002/

"Gender Ideology Harms Children." *American College of Pediatricians*, 14 Sept. 2017, www.acpeds.org/the-college-speaks/position-statements/gender-ideology-harms-children

Fleming, Rex J. *The Rise and Fall of the Carbon Dioxide Theory of Climate Change.* Springer International Publishing, 2020.

Doctrines

"Position Statements." *Christian Reformed Church*, 15 Nov. 2019, www.crcna.org/welcome/beliefs/position-statements

"Book Of Discipline & Book Of Resolutions Free Versions: UMC Books." *Cokesbury,* www.cokesbury.com/book-of-discipline-book-of-resolutions-free-versions

"Articles of Faith." *Church of the Nazarene,* www.nazarene.org/articles-faith

"AG Position Papers and Other Statements." *Assemblies of God (USA) Official Web Site | AG Position Papers and Other Statements,* https://ag.org/Beliefs/Position-Papers

"Position Papers." *Missionary Church USA*, 11 Feb. 2020, www.mcusa.org/position-papers/#1

"The Discipline 2016." *Resource Center*, 6 Dec. 2019, http://resources.wesleyan.org/the-discipline-2016

"Doctrine And Polity Papers." *Doctrine-and-Polity-Papers | Church of God*, www.churchofgod.org/doctrine-and-polity-papers

"Presbyterian Church U.S.A." *Presbyterian Church U.S.A.*, http://index. pcusa.org/

"BELIEFS." *Evangelical Presbytarian Churches,* http://epc.org/about/ beliefs/

"ABCUSA." *ABCUSA - American Baptist Churches USA*, www.abc-usa. org/policy-statements-and-resolutions/

"The 2015 Book of Discipline of the Free Methodist Church - USA." *Free Methodist Church USA*, http://fmcusa.org/resources/2015bo dforeward/2015bodch3